WITH THE
41ST DIVISION
IN THE
SOUTHWEST PACIFIC

Photograph of the author after his discharge in January 1946.
His uniform was bare when he left the service. His mother
and his aunt, wanting him to have the ribbons and stripes and
patches for this photograph, took his discharge to a military
supply store and purchased the appropriate items.

WITH THE
41ST DIVISION
IN THE
SOUTHWEST
PACIFIC

A Foot Soldier's Story

FRANCIS B. CATANZARO

INDIANA University Press

Bloomington & Indianapolis

This book is a publication of
Indiana University Press
601 North Morton Street
Bloomington, Indiana 47404-3797 USA

ISBN 0-253-34142-6

To the Men of Company I
162nd Infantry

CONTENTS

FOREWORD

In exotic, steamy, coral-encrusted jungle locales throughout the southern and western Pacific, American soldiers once fought for their lives against a tough, powerful enemy. When war broke out in 1941 between the United States and Japan, most Americans had never even heard of Hollandia, Biak, and Mindanao, places where Francis "Bernie" Catanzaro and his 41st Infantry Division buddies fought in World War II. The same, unfortunately, was true upon the war's conclusion three and a half years later. When the average American thought of the Pacific War, he or she thought of Marine-dominated battles such as Guadalcanal, Tarawa, Saipan, Guam, Iwo Jima, and Okinawa. The Army's considerable role in the defeat of Japan was shadowy, almost anonymous—a real irony, because the Army did the majority of the ground fighting in the war against Japan.

The Central Pacific campaigns of Admiral Chester Nimitz enjoyed most of the Pacific War notoriety from correspondents and posterity from historians. These battles were fought in fairly accessible areas, with the dramatic assistance of great fleets. They were spearheaded by the Marine Corps, which is, by necessity, the most publicity-conscious branch of the American armed forces. Central Pacific battles were the highest American priority in the Pacific War, probably because of the geographic reality that control of this area facilitated a direct approach to the Japanese home islands for American ships, planes, and ground troops.

General Douglas MacArthur's Southwest Pacific campaigns received, much to his chagrin, close to the lowest priority of the entire American war effort. Throughout the entire war, MacArthur struggled fiercely for the necessary soldiers, weapons, equipment, and supplies he believed he needed to fulfill his greatest goal—

returning to the Philippines. He usually had to settle for the left-overs. His men fought small battles, but long campaigns in New Guinea from 1942 to 1944, in almost total anonymity. Any head-lines for these campaigns normally went to MacArthur, a military glory hound whose zeal for publicity rivaled personalities such as George Patton and Bernard Montgomery. Dispatches and news re-leases from MacArthur's headquarters almost always featured his name and his name only. Rarely did any of his subordinate com-manders receive much credit; nor did his soldiers—the ones who endured terrible heat, tropical diseases, and hair-raising danger to win him his victories.

For two years, these GIs, mostly members of units such as the 32nd and 41st Infantry Divisions, fought their way across the for-bidding northern coast of New Guinea. By the spring of 1944, Gen-eral MacArthur was poised to clear out the entire northwest coast of this massive island. This area, once loosely controlled by Dutch colonial authorities, was now home to well over 100,000 Japanese soldiers. MacArthur and his staff knew that they did not have the kind of soldiers and resources to destroy all Japanese resistance on New Guinea. They merely hoped to control strategic points along the coast, along with several nearby islands, while bypassing thou-sands of enemy troops who were left to starve while the American war machine advanced onward to the Philippines. To that end, the Americans decided to outflank the main Japanese troop concentra-tions in Wewak and Hansa Bay, on the north coast of New Guinea. MacArthur's invasion force of 80,000 soldiers, supported by 217 ships, would leapfrog all the way to Hollandia, once Japanese air strength there had been destroyed by General George Kenney's 5th Air Force. MacArthur could do this because he knew, from ULTRA intelligence information, the exact dispositions of Japanese forma-tions in northwest New Guinea. As a result, MacArthur's Hollandia operation, executed in April 1944, was, in the opinion of Ed Drea, the leading historian of World War II intelligence gathering, "the classic example of the application of intelligence from codebreak-ing to operational planning in World War II."[1]

When soldiers from the 41st Infantry Division invaded Hum-

1. Drey, *MacArthur's ULTRA,* p. 121.

boldt Bay near Hollandia on April 22nd, they encountered almost no resistance, at least by the standards of the Pacific War. Mac-Arthur's effective use of intelligence produced this happy result for the assault troops, who dealt mainly with scattered groups of frightened, demoralized Japanese rear area troops. The combat soldiers of Japan's 18th Army were, meanwhile, waiting far to the east at Wewak and Hansa Bay. They were trapped, checkmated, consigned to a sharp but ultimately futile counterattack at Aitape, east of Hollandia. The Americans had trapped them. The 41st Division pushed westward from Hollandia, deep into the jungle, along small trails, until they joined hands on April 26th with the 24th Infantry Division moving from the other direction.

The going was much tougher for the 41st Division (Jungleers) a month later when they attacked Biak, a small, strategically located island near the extreme northwest coast of New Guinea. More than 12,000 well-entrenched Japanese soldiers defended Biak. They made ingenious use of ideal terrain for defenders. A coral ridge dominated the entire invasion coast of Biak. Here the Japanese dug or burrowed themselves into bunkers, pillboxes, tunnels, and caves. They made especially effective use of the latter terrain feature. Caves literally honeycombed the place. Within them, small units of Japanese resisted ferociously. They supported one another with interlocking fields of fire. They built ledges that helped them survive satchel charges and sometimes even flamethrower attacks. They fought to the death.

MacArthur expected a three-day campaign to seize Biak, but he vastly underestimated the strength and resolve of Japanese resistance. Nor did he appreciate the challenges of the terrain. When soldiers from the 162nd and 186th Regiments (two of the three regiments composing the 41st Division) splashed ashore (after the Navy fired almost 2,500 shells in a pre-invasion bombardment), they found themselves pinned down in small pockets along the coast. The Japanese poured withering fire down on them from the coral ridge paralleling the coast. Through sheer toughness and resolve, they pushed their way inland by reconnoitering blind alley jungle trails. Step by bloody step, they captured small pieces of the island, the ultimate objective being the Mokmer Airfield. American commanders wanted Mokmer and a couple of other nearby airfields for use in the mid-June offensive in the Mariana Islands, the centerpiece Pacific theater operation in 1944.

However, American commanders knew that Mokmer could not be taken (or held) without control of the ridges and caves overlooking the airdrome. Accomplishing this took several days of hard and agonizing fighting for the Americans. MacArthur even sent one of his most trusted commanders, Lieutenant General Robert Eichelberger, to oversee the Biak operation. Eichelberger replaced his West Point classmate, Major General Horace Fuller, at Biak. Fuller, feeling that his immediate superior, Lieutenant General Walter Krueger, did not fully or fairly appreciate the situation on Biak, actually requested to be relieved. Eichelberger tried to dissuade Fuller from doing so, but he would have none of it.

Eichelberger did inject some semblance of new life into the American effort at Biak. His GIs established control of most of Mokmer in addition to fighting off some fierce Japanese counterattacks. Once the Americans gained control of the airfields on Biak, the battle turned into a perilous, but steady, cleanup operation to destroy Japanese "pockets of resistance." This term referred primarily to the Ibdi Pocket, located roughly in the middle of the coral ridge overlooking the sea, along with two extensive networks of caves known as the West Caves and the East Caves. The Jungleers roasted and blasted the Japanese out of the West and East Caves by Independence Day. Just over two weeks later, on July 22nd, they captured the last of the Ibdi Pocket. Even so, fighting continued until the final days of August, as isolated groups of Japanese fought to the end.

Thus, what MacArthur had expected would be a three-day battle had instead turned into a three-month struggle. In that sense, Biak was similar to another campaign fought to pave the way to the Philippines—Peleliu. The ferocity of combat, level of resistance, and loss of life were greater on Peleliu, of course, but the comparison still holds. At both places, American commanders anticipated a quick victory, only to discover a stunning level of enemy resistance. Before the Americans knew it, they were drawn into a bloody, protracted fight that was little more than glorified butchery. Moreover, the Japanese used similar tactics on Peleliu and Biak, resisting the invasion at the waterline, but not to the point of expending their reserves in a vain effort to push the Americans into the sea. The Japanese used the terrain to their advantage, forcing the Americans to blast them out of a dizzying network of caves and ridges. The enemy also avoided costly and foolish banzai charges. They realized by now that such charges, stemming from the Japanese belief in Ya-mato Damashii (or fighting spirit), played right into American hands, allowing them to use their considerable firepower with devastating effectiveness and a minimum of casualties, albeit a maximum of pri-mal fear. Now, after two years of war, the Japanese preferred instead to remain on the defensive while inflicting as many casualties on the Americans as they could—an effective strategy, and a chilling pre-cursor to bitter, costly battles such as Iwo Jima or Okinawa.

Without any doubt, Biak was the toughest campaign for the 41st Division in World War II. In the course of the war, the outfit lost more than 1,000 men killed in action, 400 of whom lost their lives at Biak. Another 2,000 men from the division were wounded at Biak. The division also suffered a staggering 7,000 "nonbattle" casualties, victims of combat fatigue or sickness. Even had there been no Japanese resistance, the equatorial conditions alone posed a great challenge. Temperatures ranged well into the 100s. Mosqui-toes thrived in the jungles of Biak. The place crawled with tropical life. The climate led to jungle rot, a painful skin ailment that could only be treated with smelly, orange-colored ointment. Scrub typhus and malaria took a heavy toll on the GIs. Even a vast array of shots and pills could not prevent men from getting sick. Thousands had to be evacuated, while thousands more fought the Japanese day after day in spite of high fever, cold chills, or diarrhea.

Because of the awful bloodletting at Biak, the division needed the rest of the year to replenish its ranks and prepare for further combat. The unit sat by and licked its wounds while MacArthur's legions returned to the Philippines, first at Leyte in October 1944, and then at the main island of Luzon in January 1945. When the 41st did become combat ready again in February 1945, MacArthur assigned it to a supporting role in the Philippines campaign, namely helping to clear out the southern portion of the archipel-ago. On March 10, 1945, the 162nd and 163rd Infantry Regiments assaulted the extreme southwestern tip of the island of Mindanao, near a city called Zamboanga. Among the sizable islands of the Philippines, Mindanao was located farthest to the south.

Aided by Filipino guerillas, the Americans quickly captured Zamboanga and its nearby coastal plain. Once again the Japanese put the terrain to good use, making a stand a few miles inland at Mount Capisan, the dominant geographic feature of the whole area. The fighting centered around control of this mountain. Basically, the Jungleers hacked their way through thick jungle each day, killing off any Japanese they encountered, while engineers built a road behind them. Overhead, Marine aircraft provided skillful close air support. Every night, the infantrymen set up perimeters. The Japanese tried desperately to infiltrate the American perimeters. They wanted to get into the foxholes and cut the throats of individual American soldiers. All night long, one man in each foxhole was awake, watching and listening. Plain and simple, anyone moving in the perimeter without authorization got shot.

For two weeks the fighting raged in this manner. Finally, on March 25th, the 162nd Infantry subdued the last Japanese at Mount Capisan. Japanese resistance then noticeably softened. The enemy troops were cut off from their supply bases, stranded in hostile territory, looking to fight to the death or escape somehow. The fighting on the Zamboanga peninsula now turned into a hunting expedition of sorts. American patrols, working closely with Filipino guerillas, roamed around the peninsula looking for enclaves of Japanese resistance. By early April, the Japanese were finished. They had lost more than 6,000 men. For the rest of the war, the 41st Division participated mostly in small operations designed to clear out little islands or provide support for other American units. The combat soldiers endured the usual privations—bad food, filth, heat, fatigue, diseases—but not quite as many dangers as the summer before. In early August, they were overjoyed to hear of the atomic bombings of Hiroshima and Nagasaki. Maybe the Japanese would surrender, and they would not have to invade Japan itself. On August 14, 1945[2] their hopes became reality.

The campaigns in which Bernie Catanzaro (affectionately known to his comrades as "Zero") fought were not glamorous. They were fought in backwater places, amid horrendous condi-

2. August 15th for Bernie, who was on the other side of the international date line.

tions, in near anonymity. There were no joyous crowds cheering their liberators. No girls streaming forth to plant kisses on the cheeks of smiling soldiers. No wine and beer flowing in paved streets. No food and shelter offered to liberators. Actually, there was hardly any civilization to speak of; American soldiers like Catanzaro mostly saw jungles, caves, and coral. Their existence was austere, their circumstances remote.

They found themselves thousands of miles away from home, and the distance seemed every bit that great because they lived in a world that had nothing in common with their homeland. There was a constant sense of isolation, as if time, and perhaps the folks back home, had forgotten them. Mail service was slow, beer rations were warm, and hot, nutritious food was a rarity. In essence, they turned into jungle explorers for two or three years, divorcing themselves from the usual comforts and advantages of American life. Most mid-twentieth-century Americans traced their lineage to Europe. They could relate to and understand the liberation of old towns in France, Belgium, Italy, or Holland. By contrast, the "liberation" of small patches of faceless jungle did not make much of an impression, even though that liberation required just as much sacrifice. Perhaps that lack of empathy, more than anything else, accounts for the enduring obscurity of the Army's Pacific War.

Campaigns such as Hollandia, Biak, and Zamboanga will probably remain overshadowed by the bigger, more glamorous American battles of World War II, but they are well worth remembering—if not for the places, then for the people who won them. Men like Bernie Catanzaro once laid their lives on the line for their country, and that should never be forgotten. I met him quite by coincidence at a local car dealership. We were both having our cars serviced. We sat across from each other, reading in the waiting room. I was, ironically enough, reading a book on the campaign in the Philippines. He saw my book and mentioned that he had once fought in the Philippines. We struck up a conversation, and in the course of it he said that he had written a memoir about his experiences. He was, he told me, motivated to write by the anonymity of the campaigns in which he had fought. He thought that the story of those campaigns should be told by someone who was there, and he is 100 percent correct. It should be.

I read his memoir and was immediately impressed with his modesty and powers of description. What follows on the succeeding pages is a clear, concise, perceptive, well-written description of what it was actually like to fight with I Company, 3rd Battalion, 162nd Infantry Regiment, 41st Division in World War II, from Hollandia through the Philippines. Only a tiny handful of memoirs from this corner of the war have been written, so Bernie's story is long overdue. He makes no attempt to glorify his own actions; nor does he shrink from the unpleasant realities of combat or his reaction to it.

He was a typical, ordinary dogface GI, unremarkable in so many ways, an Italian American kid from St. Louis who signed up and did his part for the war effort. He served at the very cutting edge of battle, as a rifleman in a rifle company. There was no job more dangerous in the U.S. Army in World War II. He was a solid, dependable young man—steady, imperturbable, sensible, and reliable. In that respect, he was similar to so many others who fought for the United States in World War II. He was an ordinary man doing extraordinary things in extraordinary times. When the war ended, he came home, left the Army, and went on with his life. But the war affected the rest of his life, and he carried it with him, like so many other veterans, forever after. You could not spend two years of your life in the Pacific—going the entire time without a hot shower—and expect otherwise.

Bernie, like many other American veterans, felt the urge to record his experiences. Those who were not there might never be able to truly understand combat (only experience provides such understanding), but they should certainly know as much as possible about it. His story, then, should be seen as something of a microcosm. It is the story not just of a 19-year-old rifleman, but of so many other Americans in combat in the Pacific. Truly, Bernie Catanzaro was the very embodiment of the American combat soldier in World War II.

John C. McManus
author of *The Deadly Brotherhood:
The American Combat Soldier in
World War II*

PREFACE

After World War II had come to an end and I was back at home, I seldom talked about my service in the U.S. Army. I was happy to be a civilian again, and I tried to put my experiences as an infantryman out of my mind. However, there were infrequent occasions over the years, usually while talking with others who had served, when the war was the subject of our conversations. During those discussions, as we traded war stories, I would often say, "I should write a book about my life as a foot soldier." The statement was always made facetiously; however, as the years passed and retirement became a reality, I began to seriously consider doing so. With the encouragement of my wife, Jayne, one July afternoon when it was too hot to work in my garden, I took a ruled notebook from my desk drawer, picked up a pencil, and began to write.

My primary goal, as I began, was to tell the story of my life as an infantryman during the war. Because about 80 percent of my army life was spent as a member of Company I, 162nd Infantry, my story and the story of Company I are inseparable. The setting for most of the story is the Southwest Pacific.

Although it has been more than fifty years since my discharge from the U.S. Army, some memories are still quite vivid; others, however, have been dimmed by the passing years. To help me recall the sequence of events, I used the letters that I wrote home during the war. My family had saved every letter I wrote to them, numbering 125 in all. The letters mailed from overseas were all censored and did not contain any military information. To avoid needlessly worrying my family, I purposely did not write anything about what happened during combat. I tried to assure everyone that I was well and that there was no need for undue concern about me.

In addition to those letters, I also have a scrapbook containing photographs taken during the war, some by me and some by other GIs. The scrapbook also contains magazine and newspaper articles about the 41st Infantry Division. My grandfather, Bernard Villardi, with whom I shared a room after my grandmother's death, had collected the clippings during the war. The books *The Jungleers: A History of the 41st Infantry Division* by William F. McCartney and *41st Infantry Division: Fighting Jungleers* by Hargis Westerfield were helpful references, as were the official U.S. Army, Navy and Air Force histories.

Because the joint chiefs of staff had assigned a status of third priority to the Southwest Pacific behind the European and Central Pacific theaters, little has been written about the army's battles in New Guinea and the southern Philippines. In my search of the local library shelves, I found numerous books written by and about marines and their battles in the Central Pacific, but I found only two books written by anyone who took part in the campaigns fought by our division. Both books were written by General Robert Eichelberger, commander of the Eighth Army. In the preface of the official U.S. Army history, *The Approach to the Philippines,* author Robert Ross Smith writes about the lack of contemporary historical coverage of those battles.

> Unlike most operations in the Central Pacific and in Europe, those of the U.S. Army ground combat forces in the Southwest Pacific Area had no contemporary historical coverage during World War II. In the last named theater, no teams of historians accompanied combat units to observe, collect materials, conduct interviews, and prepare preliminary historical manuscripts. Thus the sections of this volume concerning operations in the Southwest Pacific Area are based primarily upon the official unit records maintained during combat and to a lesser extent, the unit After Action Reports required by Army regulations.

I learned in the first few weeks after my return home that the army's part in the war in the Southwest Pacific was not widely publicized. While renewing acquaintances, I found that most persons knew little or nothing about the places where we had fought. When I talked about taking part in assault landings, I learned that many people thought that the landings in the Pacific were made by the marines and that the army came ashore only after the beachheads had been secured. I hope that these pages will help dispel such misinformation. A paragraph on the dust cover of General Eichelberger's book *Our Jungle Road to Tokyo* addresses the role of the U.S. Army in the Pacific War.

> Many of us think of the Pacific War as a series of sea and air battles and amphibious Marine actions. But from the bloody, sweating jungles of Buna, just across the way from Australia to the avenues of Yokohama, it was predominantly the Army's war: a war of divisions and corps and, most of all, of mud-spattered, dog-tired, fever-wracked, overloaded, underfed men who plodded through thousands of miles for three long agonizing years.

While doing research on the campaigns in New Guinea and the Philippines, I learned facts about those battles of which I had been unaware, even though I took part in the fighting. I have used some of that information to reinforce my memory of what took place so that I might tell the story with as much historical accuracy as possible.

As I began to record the events, I quickly discovered that writing was not easy, at least for me. Although I never expected that anyone other than my relatives and friends would read my story, I wanted to make it as interesting as possible. More important, though, I wanted it to be a true story of the life of a foot soldier, so I tried to include the dull, daily routine as well as the excitement and terror of combat. As I recorded some of the happenings, I began to distrust my memory, but I have tried diligently to relate the story as it took place. The account is lacking in direct quotations that would have added interest, but the passing of the years has erased the exact words of most of those conversations. If there are errors or exaggerations in the following pages, they are inadvertent.

I have endeavored to relate the misery, tension, cruelty, and terror of combat without being too explicit. I decided that there was little to be gained by relating in detail the destruction of human bodies by bullets and exploding shells. I have tried to write a story about the war that my grandchildren could read and enjoy but from which they could also learn something about the horrors of war.

Because fifty years have passed and many things in our world have changed, I feel that I should explain my use of the terms "Japs" and "Nips" to describe the Japanese soldiers. I know that the terms are considered disparaging today, and I have not used them to degrade the Japanese people, but I did not feel that I could honestly tell the story without the use of those terms. We, who fought the enemy, did not call them Japanese; they were Japs or Nips to us. I do not think that most of us felt that the terms were derogatory, but if we had known that, I am certain that it would not have prevented us from using them. Undoubtedly, we and the Japanese harbored feelings of contempt and hatred for each other. Although the passage of fifty years has softened the feelings I held at that time, it has not completely erased them.

ACKNOWLEDGMENTS

My thanks are due my dear wife, Jayne, who has served as an editor and critic, attempting to rectify my errors in grammar and punctuation while offering encouragement and assistance with this endeavor.

I am also very grateful to my daughter-in-law, Patty, for her patience while organizing, typing, and incorporating the countless changes I have made to this manuscript. Without her perseverance and computer skills, this book could not have come about.

John Maier, William Magnan, Harry Levins, Jerry Cooper, Stephen Taaffe, and Vernon Thurmer have read all or parts of my manuscript and have offered suggestions and encouragement.

My thanks are also due Robert Sloan, senior sponsoring editor at Indiana University Press, for his kindness and support. Kendra Stokes, assistant sponsoring editor, has also been most helpful in supplying information and advice concerning the publication process. Thanks also to Jane Lyle, managing editor, and to Tony Brewer, assistant managing editor, for their help.

Finally, I appreciate the time and effort expended by John McManus while writing the excellent foreword for this book.

CHRONOLOGY

June 1943
   21 Inducted into the U.S. Army; Jefferson Barracks, St. Louis, Missouri.
July 1943
    5 First day of active duty; Jefferson Barracks.
    8 Departed Jefferson Barracks aboard troop train; destination unknown.
   13 Arrived Camp Roberts, California.
December 1943
   22 Departed Camp Roberts by train; destination home.
   26 Arrived home.
   31 Departed home by train; destination Fort Ord, California.
January 1944
    4 Arrived Fort Ord.
   13 Departed Fort Ord by train, then ferry, and arrived at Fort McDowell, Angel Island, California.
   17 Departed Fort McDowell by ferry and arrived at Camp Knight, Oakland, California.
   31 Returned to Fort McDowell by ferry.
February 1944
    6 Departed Fort McDowell by ferry to Oakland. Boarded *USAT Sea Corporal,* which departed in late afternoon; destination unknown.
   23 Landed at Brisbane, Australia.
   28 Departed Brisbane by train and arrived at Rockhampton, Australia.
March 1944
   24 Departed Rockhampton by truck. Arrived at Gladstone and boarded cargo ship that departed that afternoon; destination unknown.
April 1944
    3 Landed at Finschhafen, New Guinea.
   19 Boarded LCI for invasion of Hollandia, Dutch New Guinea.
   22 Made assault landing at H+15 minutes on White Beach 1 at Humboldt Bay, Hollandia.
May 1944
   25 Boarded LCI; destination Biak Island, Dutch New Guinea.
   27 Made assault landing at H+30 minutes at Bosnek, Biak Island.

August 1944
  15   Departed Biak by LCM and arrived at hospital on Owi Island.
  16   Departed Owi on C-47 cargo plane; arrived at hospital in Hollandia.
September 1944
  3   Boarded LST for return trip to Biak.
  5   Arrived at Biak.
January 1945
  20   Boarded troop transport; destination unknown.
February 1945
  3   Landed on Mindoro Island, Philippines.
March 1945
  8   Boarded LST; destination Zamboanga, Mindanao.
  10   Made assault landing in first wave at Zamboanga.
May 1945
  3   Boarded LST; destination Parang, Mindanao.
  4   Landed at Parang.
  10   Boarded LST; destination Davao area.
  11   Landed at Digos, Mindanao.
  31   Boarded LCM for series of four commando-type landings in Davao
       Gulf area.
June 1945
  6   Returned to Davao area.
  10   Began move to front; objective Calinan, Mindanao.
July 1945
  3   Boarded LST for return to Zamboanga.
September 1945
  19   Boarded troop transport; destination Kure and Hiroshima, Japan.
October 1945
  6   Arrived in Kure Bay and occupied submarine base at Kure.
  20   Rode on top of barracks bags in Japanese truck with two Japanese sol-
       diers to Fukuyama, Japan.
December 1945
  22   Boarded train; destination Nagoya, Japan.
  23   Arrived Nagoya.
  29   Boarded troop transport *USS Admiral H. T. Mayo;* destination San
       Francisco.
January 1946
  10   Arrived San Francisco. Boarded ferry to Camp Stoneman at Pittsburg,
       California.
  13   Boarded train; destination Jefferson Barracks, St. Louis, Missouri.
  17   Arrived Jefferson Barracks.
  18   Received Honorable Discharge and rode city bus home.

WITH THE
41ST DIVISION
IN THE
SOUTHWEST PACIFIC

1

Basic Training
Camp Roberts

The streets were deserted. It was 5:45 on the morning of July 5, 1943. I was about to begin my first day of active service in the U.S. Army. I had been instructed by the Selective Service Board to report to the acting corporal at the Broadway entrance of Jefferson Barracks, St. Louis, Missouri, at 6:45 A.M. Because it was the Monday following the 4th of July, most people were celebrating the last day of the three-day weekend by sleeping late. I felt that I was already making a sacrifice for my country as I walked to the bus stop.

Using a token that had been sent to me by the draft board, I boarded the Chippewa bus and transferred to the Broadway streetcar and the Barracks bus. The acting corporal was waiting, troop roster in hand, at the barracks gate.

Following an orientation talk and a personal interview with a placement officer, the first order of business was a visit to the camp barber shop. After my fellow inductees and I had been properly shorn, which took no more than three minutes per man, we were sent to the supply sergeant to be outfitted. We received fatigue uniforms, underwear, socks, and shoes. Although I wore a size 10AA shoe as a civilian, a GI, after measuring my feet, handed me a pair of size 9B boots. I wisely said nothing and in fact wore the boots for more than a year with no problems whatsoever.

I was a teenager, and as I prepared to spend my first night in an army barracks, I looked forward with excitement and anticipation to the days ahead. During my interview with the placement officer, he informed me that my score on the AGCT (Army General Classification Test) I had taken on the day of my induction was very high. He assured me that a good spot would be found for me in the U.S. Army.

I had not long to wait to find out what that "good spot" would be. I found my name on a list of those scheduled to ship out on July 8th. On the afternoon of the designated day, about fifty fellow soldiers and I boarded two old Pullman cars sitting on a siding at the Barracks. Shortly afterward, the cars were coupled to other cars and the train pulled out of the station. It was the beginning of the first of many "all expense paid trips" I would take during my two and a half years of army service.

At that time, troop movements were carried out in great secrecy, but rumors about our destination abounded. The journey started in a southerly direction; it was "obvious" that we were headed for a camp in Arkansas. However, by the next morning we had crossed Arkansas and were stopped at the station in Texarkana, Texas. Now everyone was certain that a training camp in Texas would be our destination.

While the train was stopped at the station, we were allowed to get off to stretch our legs. At that time we learned that we were not the only military personnel aboard the train. Three Pullman cars occupied by WACs (Women's Army Corps) were a part of the train. This discovery held promise to change a rather dull journey into one much more interesting. However, shortly after we got back aboard the train, our hopes were quickly dashed. The lieutenant in charge of our group firmly informed us that the cars occupied by the WACs were off limits to us, as were our cars to them. We never saw any of those WACs again.

After three days and two nights crossing the Lone Star State, much of the time with the train sitting on sidings, we reached the New Mexico border. It seemed certain that our destination was either New Mexico or Arizona. When we reached Yuma, Arizona, at the end of the fourth day, it was apparent that we were California bound. As we pulled out of the Yuma station in late afternoon, I noticed an Indian sitting on a blanket on the platform. A large thermometer hanging on a post nearby indicated a temperature of 114°F.

On the morning of the fifth day of the journey, the train pulled into Union Station in Los Angeles, where we transferred to another train. That afternoon we arrived at our destination, Camp Roberts, situated amid the barren coastal hills about midway between Los Angeles and San Francisco along U.S. Highway 101. The closest towns were Paso Robles and San Miguel.

Camp Roberts, the largest army replacement training center in the United States, covered an area of fifty-eight square miles. Its white wooden buildings with green shingled roofs were clustered around a huge parade ground. The camp, resembling a small town, had numerous facilities, including post exchanges, service clubs, theaters, dispensaries, infirmaries, barber shops, a laundry, a sports arena, a post office, and a guest house. Nine chapels, which were staffed by twenty-four chaplains representing most religious denominations, afforded camp occupants the opportunity to practice their religions. I was assigned to Company C of the 78th Battalion for training as a rifleman. It seemed that my "good spot," at least for the immediate future, would be in the infantry.

Basic training, we learned, would last for fourteen weeks and would begin immediately. I was assigned a bunk on the second floor of the company barracks, where I prepared to spend the first night of my stay at Camp Roberts. It was a stay that would last for about five months.

My first big surprise was the weather at Camp Roberts. Because it was mid-July, the days were extremely hot, but what was so amazing to a St. Louisan accustomed to hot summer nights was the big drop in the temperature that began as soon as the sun sank below the horizon. On that first night, I was surprised to find two olive-drab woolen blankets at the foot of my bunk. We slept with the windows wide open, and by morning I had pulled both of the blankets over me. I was happy to have them.

I slept soundly that first night at camp, and I was not ready to hit the floor when we were all awakened by the corporal at 0500 the next morning. We soon learned that there was no time to waste if we were to be ready for the order to fall out for reveille, which usually took place at 0530.

After the reveille formation and a substantial breakfast, we lined up at the supply building, where we were issued equipment and clothing to supplement what we had received at Jefferson Barracks. It was at that time that I received "the best friend of an infantryman," my rifle. My "best friend" was a shiny M1 Garand that accompanied me during almost every exercise of basic training. The idea that our rifles were our best friends and that we should treat them as such was drilled into us continually. Anyone unlucky enough to drop his piece, as it was usually called, was ordered to keep it with him at all times until he learned to treat it properly. This meant that the unfortunate individual took his rifle to bed with him and to any place he went while awake, including visits to the latrine and the mess hall. It was not unusual to see a GI eating with a fork in one hand and his rifle in the other.

After more than fifty years, my memories of basic training are not sharp enough to relate every incident in chronological order, but most of the major events are still quite vivid in my mind. I remember that on my first weekend in camp, when most of the men were enjoying a day and a half of leisure, I drew KP (kitchen police) duty for the first time. I learned quickly that anyone whose surname started with a letter near the beginning of the alphabet would be among the first chosen when detail lists were compiled.

One day shortly after the beginning of our training, the corporal, who was a member of the training cadre for our company, talked to us about the difficulty of the weeks ahead. He predicted that some of us would not be able to complete the program but that those who did would be in the best physical condition of their lives. He guaranteed that the men who were too heavy would lose weight and that those who were too light would gain the pounds they needed. His predictions proved to be amazingly accurate. By the end of basic, twenty-five of the sixty-five men in our barracks were either discharged or reassigned to less demanding service. Most of those who could not meet the requirements were older men, those thirty and above. The men who were overweight also had a difficult time. Those who completed the program were in great shape on graduation day. The heavy men had slimmed down, and the skinny guys had put on needed pounds. As a 19-year-old I was 5'8" tall and weighed 118 pounds when training started; I weighed a solid 149 pounds on graduation day. In a letter to my sister Margaret, I wrote, "It doesn't seem like thirty is an old age, but it is really tough going for the older guys. Their legs just don't want to carry them. This army, especially the infantry, is for young men."

The days during basic training were long, hot, physically demanding, and at times very boring. The nights always seemed to be too short. Lights out was usually at 2100, but many of us were often in our bunks before that hour. We were allowed to stay out until 2300, but, except for Saturday nights, very few of us ever did. We knew that the wakeup call the next morning would be at 0500 or sometimes even earlier. We usually trained until 1800, but at times there were night marches or other night-training exercises.

A normal week consisted of five days of training followed by a Saturday morning inspection and dress parade. The Saturday morning parades took place on the infantry parade ground, the largest in the country. The camp band usually played as we drilled and marched in review. Saturday afternoons and Sundays were off days unless a person had been unlucky enough to draw KP or guard duty. I can recall at least three weekends that I spent on KP while I was at Camp Roberts. Although most of our company was made up of men from St. Louis, there were some from other areas. On weekends when passes were available, some of the men from California went home, but most of us stayed in camp attending church services, taking in a movie, or just lounging in our bunks. To get away from camp for an afternoon, it was possible to take a bus to San Miguel or Paso Robles. Round-trip fares were twenty cents to San Miguel and thirty cents to Paso Robles. I recall going to Paso Robles twice and to San Miguel once.

I don't remember much about the quality of food at camp, but I do know that I never left the mess hall feeling hungry. In a letter to my mother, I wrote, "My breakfast this morning included corn flakes, two eggs, fried potatoes, pork sausage, bread, butter, milk, and an orange. We usually have potatoes three times a day. I eat anything and everything." The arduous days made it imperative to stoke up at every opportunity. On most evenings, I walked to the PX (post exchange) after supper to buy a bedtime snack, a pint of ice cream and a bag of cookies, which I usually consumed while lounging on my bunk.

There were only a few routine medical exams or treatments that I recall. Of course, there was a schedule for periodic inoculations. These shots were usually followed by calisthenics with a lot of arm exercises that we were told would minimize the soreness from the shots. I remember well the first of our routine "short-arm" (venereal disease) exams. The sergeant ordered us to fall out in a uniform of raincoat and boots. I had heard the saying, "The right way, the wrong way, and the army way," so I was not about to question the sergeant. I could not imagine the reason for such a bizarre uniform, but I fell out dressed as ordered. An unfortunate few who wore socks with their boots were none-too-gently chewed out by the sergeant. He informed them that a uniform of raincoat and boots did not include socks, underwear, or anything else.

We wore boots without socks because foot exams were usually carried out in conjunction with the short-arm exams. For an infantryman, of course, good foot care was essential. We were told to keep our feet clean, to wear clean socks, to use foot powder, and to keep our toenails trimmed. Each of us had two pairs of boots, and we were instructed not to wear the same pair on successive days.

Once during basic training I needed some nonroutine medical care. During a physical training exercise called horse and riders, I was riding on the shoulders of one of my comrades when I was pulled off from behind by another rider. As I landed, the back of my head hit a sharp rock. A few minutes later, I found myself holding a bloody rag to my head as I walked to the first aid station with a buddy at my side. I had no recollection of the accident at all.

When we reached the aid station, a doctor examined me and said that I needed stitches to close the cut. He told me to report to the camp hospital, but first I had to pack all my belongings and turn them in at the supply room. This took considerable time and effort because all my gear was on the second floor of the barracks. After I had completed turning in my gear, I was driven to the hospital. After an assistant X-rayed my head, a doctor closed the wound with several stitches. The nurse told me that I had suffered a concussion, and although I was feeling better, she ordered me to stay in bed. I spent three days in the hospital before I was released to rejoin my outfit.

The training that we received was both thorough and extensive.

Each hour of every day was scheduled with varied training activities. Hurry up and wait was to be expected in the army; however, during basic training I can recall a lot of hurrying but very little waiting. We would usually spend any spare time between training exercises policing the company street and the area around the barracks. I particularly disliked picking up the cigarette butts that littered the ground.

The sergeant in charge of our training and the corporal who assisted him accompanied us on all training activities. The sergeant was tough but fair. Those who screwed up were chewed out and paid the price by serving extra duty, but we quickly learned that if we followed orders we had nothing to fear. I don't remember that anyone was ever cursed; we were always addressed as "soldier." In off hours the sergeant stayed apart from the trainees; but the corporal, a dark-skinned, bright-eyed Mexican American, often socialized with us. He was a small man who always seemed to wear a smile, but he was as tough as they come. He made the training exercises look easy. I especially remember the ease with which he ran the obstacle courses. He gave us advice and became a friend to many of us.

Because we were being trained specifically as riflemen, great emphasis was put on the care and operation of our rifles. We learned how to disassemble, clean, and reassemble our rifles. We lubricated the metal parts with machine oil and rubbed the wooden stocks with linseed oil. We were taught how to fire our weapons properly, and we learned how to use the bayonets that could be mounted on them.

Bayonet drills were near the top of my list of least favored training exercises. A bayonet drill usually lasted an hour and consisted primarily of inflicting jabs, thrusts, and butt smashes on a defenseless canvas dummy while screaming "EEEEAH!" as loudly as possible. At times the drill was concluded with hand-to-hand combat in which we chose partners and tried to throw each other to the ground.

Learning how to fire our rifles was a two-week exercise. We spent the first of those two weeks on the dry firing range. During the first part of the week, we did not use our rifles at all. Instead, we used a wooden pole equipped with simulated front and rear sights. We spent countless hours in the various firing positions, pointing our make-believe rifles at targets and properly aligning the sights on the bull's-eye. During the latter part of the week, we used our rifles to perform the same exercises while slowly squeezing the triggers of our unloaded weapons. I could not understand why we spent so much time on such a simple and straightforward task. That week on the dry firing range was surely one of the most boring weeks of basic training.

The next week we moved to the live fire range. It was a much more interesting and rewarding experience. Each day of the week started at 0400 because we had to march three miles to the range and it was necessary to get an early start so the firing schedule could be completed. We spent six days firing our M1 rifles.

The M1 was a semi-automatic rifle. After inserting a clip of eight cartridges, the operator needed only to release the safety and squeeze the trigger to fire a round. As that round was fired, some of the expanding gas from the cartridge entered a gas port. A piston was forced backward, ejecting the empty cartridge and inserting another one, which could be fired immediately by squeezing the trigger again. The rounds could be fired faster and more easily than with the old bolt-action Springfield rifle.

Because I had never had a firearm of any kind in my hands until the beginning of basic training, it was with a feeling of excitement that I prepared to fire my first shot, from the prone position, at a target 100 yards distant. With my scorekeeper at my side, I loaded my rifle and released the safety. The officer in charge at the range called out, "Ready on the right? Ready on the left? Ready on the firing line? The flag is up, the flag is waving, the flag is down. Targets up. Commence firing." I took a deep breath, exhaled, aimed my rifle, and squeezed off my first shot. Although we had been cautioned to expect a slight kick from the powerful weapon, I was surprised by the force of the recoil. I was amazed, though, when the signal from the target area announced that I had scored a bull's-eye with my first shot. Maybe, I thought, the previous week on the dry fire range had not been such a waste of time after all.

We spent the first day zeroing our rifles at different ranges. The M1 was equipped with an adjustable rear sight that could be set by each individual to obtain the greatest accuracy at various ranges. During the remainder of the week, we fired from different positions and ranges and fired for score. I cannot remember the exact scoring system, but I believe it was a 5, 4, 3, 2 system starting with 5 for a bull's-eye and decreasing to lesser scores for hits in the outer circles surrounding the bull's-eye.

The targets were manned by GIs in pits beneath the targets. After each shot, the target would be lowered and a colored marker inserted showing the exact location of the hit. The target was then raised so that the shooter and his scorekeeper could note the location of the hit and assign a score. If the shot missed the target completely, the shame was announced for all to see by the waving of "Maggie's Drawers," a red flag on a long pole.

As the week progressed, we shot from the prone, kneeling, sitting, and standing positions at 100-, 200-, and 500-yard ranges. The twenty-inch bull's-eye looked very small at 500 yards, but I remember scoring three consecutive bull's-eyes at that distance. The prone position was the easiest; the standing, the hardest. After each firing sequence, the shooter and scorekeeper exchanged positions. As the week progressed, my upper lip began to swell because my right thumb was being jammed against my lip by the kick of my rifle. The fact that I had a slightly protruding dog's tooth on the right side aggravated the problem. When the week came to an end, I was pleased to learn that I had earned a sharpshooter's medal, narrowly missing an expert's score by five points. I scored 170 points out of a possible 210. Not bad for a skinny city kid, I thought.

In addition to gaining self-confidence in my ability to fire my M1, I also gained confidence in my rifle. The M1 was an accurate, powerful weapon. We were told that a bullet from an M1 could pierce the trunk of a large tree at a distance of 500 yards. We were assured that anyone hit by a bullet fired from an M1 would be knocked down regardless of where he had been hit.

Other than KP, the only detail to which we were normally assigned was night guard duty. The first time I pulled guard in mid-August, I wore woolen gloves to keep my hands warm on a cold California night. The time passed slowly as I walked my post during the still early morning hours. Because we were to start on an eight-mile hike in the morning, I was instructed to wake our platoon leader and the company commander when I completed my rounds at 0400. Neither of the officers seemed to be happy about the early wake-up call. I rather enjoyed that part of my guard duty.

Because we were being trained as foot soldiers, marches were a major component of our scheduled training. Marches could be, and were, called at any hour of the day or night. Day marches were the most difficult because afternoon temperatures regularly exceeded 100°F, often reaching 114°F to 116°F. At times, the ground became so hot that I would not even sit down during the rest breaks. Sometimes the water in my canteen got so hot that I did not drink it. On the longer hikes, an ambulance usually followed the column of marchers to pick up and give first aid to those who dropped out. As training progressed, the length of the marches increased until we were making marches of twelve to fifteen miles with full gear. Usually we walked for fifty minutes and took a ten-minute break each hour. At times there were forced marches, during which we would do double-time for fifty yards, then march for fifty yards to reach our destination in a specified time. Many of the men disliked the marches, but I was usually happy when one was announced. I had always liked to walk; I felt that as long as we were on a march we would not be doing something much more disagreeable, such as running one of the devilish obstacle courses.

As training progressed, I became stronger and my endurance increased, but I never reached the point where all of the obstacles became easy for me to traverse, particularly when running the courses in full gear. Most of the courses were about a quarter mile in length, and we were required to run from one obstacle to the next. The obstacles included climbing ladders, walking across narrow catwalks, crossing horizontal ladders hand by hand, climbing ropes, crawling through pipes, descending rope netting, swinging on ropes over muddy pools, and making ascents and descents of varied structures. One obstacle that was always difficult for me was a smooth wooden wall about eight feet high that we were required to scale. Because I was not very tall, it was necessary for me to run at full speed and leap against the wall with one foot high enough on the wall so that I could grab the top of the wall with both hands and pull myself up to the top. Loaded down with full pack and rifle, I never found that to be easy.

On one occasion, after a long march, we started to run a particularly difficult obstacle course. I progressed fairly well until I reached a log hurdle near the end of the course. As I jumped over the logs, my trailing foot hit the top log. I made it across the hurdle with no problem other than hitting the obstacle with my foot; however, an officer who was watching ordered me to take the hurdle again. A second try ended with the same sequence of events. I finally cleared the logs on the third attempt.

After everyone had completed the course and we were seated on a hillside, we were told that several officers would run the course to show how the obstacles should be traversed. The demonstration began and the officers raced through, up, and over the obstacles; I was impressed. All went well until one of the officers fell while hurdling the same obstacle that had caused me problems. It was the officer who had ordered me to take that obstacle three times. I learned later that he had fractured his ankle.

Later in the day, our battalion officers demonstrated the correct way to cross a barbed-wire obstacle. The obstacle, a section of barbed-wire fencing, was constructed with several strands of barbed wire strung between crossed poles that formed an X at each end of the section. The fence section was approximately eight feet long, four feet high, and three feet wide. Five or six officers, including the battalion commander, all in full gear, assembled for the demonstration. The battalion commander started toward the fence at full speed. Holding his rifle parallel to the ground in both hands and with his arms extended in front of him, he threw himself face down over the fence so that his body formed a bridge over the barbed wire. Then, one at a time, his junior officers ran and jumped, landing on the back of the CO (commanding officer) with one foot and then easily clearing the barbed-wire obstacle with the other foot. Everyone was amazed and impressed with the demonstration and particularly with the guts of the CO, who by this time was having his cuts patched up by the medics. Thankfully, we were never asked to carry out that exercise.

However, one thing we did practice often was how to hit the dirt while making an advance on the enemy. We were taught to run bent over with our rifles carried in front of us, to drop to our knees, then to fall forward and land with the rifle butt against the ground to cushion our fall. Once on the ground, we were to roll to one side or the other so we would not be stationary targets.

Midway through basic training I was informed that because of my test score on the AGCT, I was eligible to apply for OCS (Officer Candidate School) or the ASTP (Army Specialized Training Program). A score of at least 110 was required for admission to OCS and 115 was needed for eligibility to ASTP. After learning more about the programs, I decided to apply for the ASTP. If I could successfully complete that program, I would be graduated as an officer and engineer. That seemed preferable to becoming a second lieutenant in the infantry. To apply, it would be necessary to take a series of tests to confirm that I was qualified for participation in the program. I took the tests and was told that I would be notified of my status before the completion of basic training. As training continued, I looked forward hopefully to a favorable result.

Close-order drill, marching in formation as a noncom (noncommissioned officer) called out the cadence and marching orders, was one of the training exercises often repeated. Our first drills were ragged, leaving much room for improvement, but as the weeks passed we became more proficient and polished. By the time training was drawing to a close, I had begun to enjoy the drills, particularly those on Saturday mornings when we wore our dress suntan uniforms rather than our usual OD (olive drab) fatigues and marched on the parade grounds to the music of the camp band. To this day, when I hear a march, I always tap my left foot on the downbeat.

Saturday parades were always preceded by inspection, including, of course, rifle inspection. KP awaited anyone unlucky enough or lazy enough to be gigged by the inspecting officer. In addition to a dirty rifle, overlooked details such as an unbuttoned pocket or an unpolished belt buckle could result in a person's name appearing on the next day's KP list. Barracks inspections also were routine. Floors, windows, stairs, and latrines were scrubbed and polished. Bunks and foot lockers were put in order, and buttons on all hanging clothing were fastened. Failure to pass meant extra duty for the entire company.

As our training progressed, we were transformed from raw recruits to polished soldiers, and we counted the days remaining on the schedule. However, when we reached the completion of our ninth week, we received some discouraging news. Basic training had been increased to seventeen weeks. Graduation day had been set back three weeks.

Training in the use of gas masks was one of the drills that was often conducted. One of those exercises consisted of entering a room filled with tear gas with your gas mask in its case carried over your shoulder. Once in the room, the speed with which you could remove your mask from its carrying case and get it properly in place over your face determined how much exposure to the gas you would suffer.

I remember well a field exercise one afternoon when our company was to advance through a smokescreen to take a hill. The screen was laid down and we advanced through the smoke and took the hill with little difficulty. The CO decided that the attack should be repeated, so we retraced our route to the bottom of the hill. We took our places, spread out in an attack formation. The smokescreen was laid down again and the second attack began. We had barely advanced into the smoke when my eyes, nose, and throat began to burn. Tears rolled down my cheeks, and I began to cough. I don't know how long it took me to think about my gas mask, but it was obviously too long. By the time I had my mask in place, I was not in condition to attack anything. The only consolation I could salvage from the exercise was that I had not been alone in failing to realize what was happening and react immediately. Most of my fellow company members were in the same shape as I, crying and coughing because of the tear gas we had inhaled. It was a lesson that I never forgot.

Although we were being trained specifically as riflemen, we did have training in the use of the other weapons of a line infantry company. We were instructed in the use of hand grenades and were given the opportunity to throw live grenades. U.S. Army grenades were manufactured with a five-second fuse. We were taught to pull the pin, release the handle, and throw the grenade on the count of three. The reason for the delay before throwing the grenade was to prevent the enemy from picking up the grenade and throwing it back at you. It did take some willpower not to hurry the count.

We also learned how to maintain and fire the carbine, the BAR (Browning automatic rifle), the air-cooled .30-caliber machine gun, the bazooka, and the 60-mm mortar. I qualified as a marksman with the BAR; because it was so heavy, it was a lot more difficult to shoot than the M1.

Training films and lectures were occasionally included in our schedule. Topics covered ranged from the operation and care of our weapons, military courtesy, and the tactics of warfare to subjects such as sanitation in the field, sex hygiene, and venereal diseases. Most of the films and lectures were very boring, but I do remember one session that started with a bang. We were gathered near an outdoor wooden grandstand that was to be used for seating during the lecture. As the first man stepped onto the grandstand a deafening explosion rang out from a pit beneath the seats. The officer who was about to lecture us had gained our attention immediately. He had a rousing introduction to his lecture on booby traps.

I was designated to carry a BAR during our camp defense drills, which could be called at any time, day or night. When the alarm was sounded, the mission of our company was to move with all haste to a position along U.S. Highway 101 about a mile and a half from our barracks. Toting the BAR, especially at double time, was difficult because of its weight, about nineteen pounds, as compared to the ten pounds of an M1 or the six pounds of a carbine.

With less than a month remaining in our training schedule, I received the welcome news that I had been accepted for the ASTP. After completing basic training, I would be enrolled at a college or university to study civil engineering for two and a half years. If I could successfully complete the program, I would graduate as a second lieutenant in the army engineering corps. This, I thought, was that "good spot" that had been previously promised to me. In a letter to my sister I wrote, "I have only three more weeks to serve in the infantry. I guess I'll live through them."

During the final weeks of basic training, exercises became more difficult and realistic. Our first exposure to live fire was on the infiltration course. Machine guns, set in fixed positions, fired live ammunition in a pattern about two and a half feet above the ground. Outfitted with weapons and full packs, we crawled under the live fire around and over obstacles that brought us closer to the live rounds. The length of the course was about seventy-five yards. From pits dug on the course, explosives were fired to simulate actual combat conditions. As we inched along through the sand and dust, we traversed obstacles of logs and sandbags. At one point it was necessary to turn over onto our backs to crawl under a barbed-wire fence. All this was carried out while trying to keep our rifles clean because there was a rifle inspection immediately at the end of the course. If your weapon did not pass inspection, you cleaned it and went through the course a second time. I was pleased when I completed the course and the inspecting officer returned my rifle to me without any negative comments.

The climax of basic training began with three weeks remaining on the training calendar. We marched into the hills of the camp and set up a "combat" field bivouac that was to last for two weeks. During that time, we slept on the ground in pup tents and participated in a series of simulated combat exercises. I was not particularly pleased with the prospect of sleeping on the ground because the area around the camp was inhabited by tarantulas. Although the large hairy spiders were quite common, I don't recall that anyone was ever bitten. Some of the men killed the spiders by shooting them with blank cartridges.

During the bivouac, we participated in a night compass course; in small groups, we made our way to several checkpoints. Our company also successfully carried out a night infiltration of the camp of Company B. The entire battalion took part in a daylight "attack," during which live artillery fire was directed over our heads. P-39 fighter planes flew over us and fired at targets in the hills ahead of us. Noncoms, hidden in the hills, fired live rounds from their rifles so close to us that several men were slightly wounded by ricocheting bullets.

During another exercise, we attacked a simulated European village. Using live ammunition, we fired at targets that appeared as we opened doors or climbed through windows. At one point, I fired live rounds with a BAR from a second-story window over the heads of fellow attackers in the street below. Then I was ordered to jump from the window to the lawn below. I recall that the butt of the BAR hit the ground with a thud as I landed. Fortunately, I had been instructed to activate the safety before jumping.

A training exercise that I remember as being especially tough was the J Range. With full gear, we forded a small stream with water about waist high. When we reached the far bank of the stream, we were ordered to put on our gas masks. Then we had to scale a very steep cliff; at one point it was necessary to pull ourselves up on ropes. It was a very hot afternoon; the temperature was well over 100°F. With my gas mask in place, it was hard for me to breathe, but with considerable difficulty I finally reached the top.

The grand finale of the two weeks was the return march to our barracks while carrying full gear, which weighed almost sixty pounds. The march started in the early morning hours and was completed by about 0900. We marched 21.3 miles in seven hours and twenty minutes without a man falling out, beating the best time of any previous outfit by twenty minutes. We immediately showered, shaved, and changed to our dress suntans. After a hearty breakfast, the two-week field exercise was completed with a dress parade and review. After dismissal, I remember that I did not feel at all tired. The many weeks of training had not been in vain.

The final week of basic training was used to review the many things we had, or should have, learned. The program was formally completed with a graduation dinner on November 6th, during which we received our diplomas. I accepted mine with a feeling of relief but also a feeling of pride and accomplishment. I was no longer a trainee. I was now a full-fledged buck private. My MOS (military occupation specialty) number, 745, identified me as a rifleman.

Within a few days I was saying good-bye to many of my buddies. Most of them were headed to a POE (port of embarkation). I was feeling quite happy but also a little guilty about my good fortune of avoiding assignment overseas as a foot soldier. I was aware that infantrymen suffered a disproportionate number of the casualties during combat. During my research for this book, I learned that although infantrymen made up only 10 percent of the U.S. Army during World War II, 70 percent of all casualties were suffered by those in front-line infantry companies.[1]

I was assigned to another barracks to await the beginning of the second semester at Pasadena Junior College at Pasadena, California. During those days of waiting, I pulled light-duty details around the camp but, in all honesty, spent a lot of time just lounging on my bunk. It was during that time that I was able to attend a musical revue starring Judy Garland at the Camp Roberts Bowl, a natural amphitheater large enough to hold the entire population of the camp.

1. Ellis, *The Sharp End*, p. 158.

Shortly after Thanksgiving, disquieting rumors about ASTP began to circulate, but nothing eventful happened until mid-December, when I was called into company headquarters and was ordered to report to the dispensary for a physical exam. I could not understand why I needed a physical to attend college, but shortly afterward I learned that a directive had been issued canceling ASTP. I was told that I would receive a fourteen-day delay en route to report to Fort Ord, California, a POE, on January 4, 1944. It appeared that I was about to follow in the footsteps of my basic training buddies. I learned recently that most of them were assigned to the 25th Division, which was stationed in New Zealand at that time. They spent almost a full year in that area before experiencing their first taste of combat on the island of Luzon.

Immediately after receiving the unhappy news about ASTP, I decided to try to get home for Christmas. I sent a telegram to my father, asking him to wire me $60 so that I could purchase train tickets. I had very little cash on hand because I usually sent most of my monthly pay home. My take-home pay, after deductions for insurance and the purchase of war bonds, was $35 per month. My father later said that the only time I wrote to him was when I needed money. It was true that when I wrote home I usually addressed my letters to my mother, sister, or aunt because they were the members of my family who wrote to me. My father, who was born in Sicily, could read and write English, but writing a letter in English was difficult for him.

The money arrived promptly, and on December 22nd I boarded a train heading for St. Louis. I did not make it home for Christmas. I remember being in Pueblo, Colorado, on Christmas Eve, and in Kansas City, Missouri, on Christmas night. During basic training we were so busy that I don't recall being homesick or lonely. The fact that I was with many others, some of whom became buddies, also helped; but on that Christmas Eve and Christmas Day, I did have a feeling of great loneliness because everyone around me was a stranger.

I arrived home the day after Christmas. A small banner with a blue star was hanging in the front window of our living room. It was the custom during the war to hang such a banner to indicate that a member of the household was serving in the armed forces. If a member of the household had been killed in service, the star in the banner was gold rather than blue.

The five days at home flew by quickly. Because it had taken four and a half days to get home, and because I was to report to Fort Ord on January 4th, I decided that I should leave home on the evening of December 31st. Many of our friends and relatives had gathered at our house that day to see me and to celebrate the coming of the New Year. Shortly after the evening meal, I said my good-byes, and with my dad and Uncle Will Bruce took the Gravois bus to Union Station. Both my dad and uncle had served in the U.S. Army in World War I. I had not told my mother that I was going overseas; she would find out soon enough. I did tell my dad and uncle that Fort Ord was a POE. I can still see my Uncle Will, a big man who was a fire department captain, with tears in his eyes as we waited for the train. My dad did better, at least outwardly.

The enormous station was packed with servicemen of every description. Some were alone; others were accompanied by friends or relatives. The station was so crowded that we had to force our way through the crowd to reach the tracks. When the train arrived, servicemen were allowed to board before the civilians. I said good-bye to my dad and uncle, put the strap of my barracks bag over my shoulder, walked along the platform, and climbed aboard the train. Every seat on the train was occupied, most by servicemen. My barracks bag on its side in the aisle served as my seat until we reached Kansas City, where I had to change trains.

During the layover of an hour or so, I visited with Kay Mulligan, a classmate of my sister, whom I had dated on a few occasions. Kay was spending the Christmas holidays with an aunt who lived in Kansas City. Kay and her aunt met me at the station and invited me to stay overnight; but I was afraid that I would be late arriving at Fort Ord and be marked AWOL (absent without leave), so I declined their offer. The time to board the train for California came quickly, and again, with my barracks bag over my shoulder, I headed down the platform. Once aboard, I found the situation a repeat of that in St. Louis—no unoccupied seats. It was not until we reached Denver that I was able to claim a seat.

As the trip progressed, it became obvious that I had made a mistake by leaving on New Year's Eve; we were making much better time on the return trip than I had on my homeward trip. We arrived in San Francisco on January 3rd, a day early. This upset me, because I could have spent another day at home and welcomed in 1944, which would prove to be an eventful year. Rather than report early, I went to a movie and then got a bunk at the USO (United Service Organization) in San Francisco and spent the night there. The charge to rent the bunk was thirty-five cents.

The next morning I boarded a train for the short ride to Fort Ord, which was situated between Monterey and Salinas. My only remembrance of Fort Ord is that of the infiltration course. It was similar to the one at Camp Roberts with machine guns and explosives, but there was one difference: the weather. It was early January, and the weather was cold and rainy. The course was a sea of mud. I was not happy to be required to crawl through that mud, but crawl I did.

After a stay of about one week at Fort Ord, I was transferred to Fort McDowell on Angel Island in San Francisco Bay. Three days after my arrival, about ten or twelve of us, probably those at the top of the alphabetical troop list, were ordered to pack our gear. We boarded a ferry that took us across the bay past Alcatraz to the Oakland pier. We expected that we were about to board a ship to begin a voyage overseas, but to our surprise we marched to Camp Knight, a small army post on the Oakland waterfront. We had received a reprieve.

The next morning we marched to a building on the dock, where each of us was handed a hammer and a bucket of nails. We were about to become soldier-carpenters. Our jobs would be building pallets that were to be used to hold supplies being loaded onto ships at the dock.

I have three memories from the time I spent at Camp Knight. First, I remember that while wielding my hammer for eight hours a day, I suffered an occasional miss. Instead of hammer-to-nailhead contact there was, at times, hammer-to-finger impact. That hurt. However, as the days passed, my carpentry skills improved and the frequency of those painful incidents decreased.

My second memory, a happy one, is of the food at Camp Knight. We ate like kings. The quality of the meals was unbelievable. As we moved through a cafeteria line, we chose from a variety of soups, salads, and vegetables. Steaks and seafood were among the many entrees offered. Desserts included cakes, pies, ice cream, and fresh fruits. Obviously, the camp had an excellent mess sergeant who had access to a tremendous variety of fresh foods from the fields of California.

My final memory from that time is of the ocean. We had evenings free, and it was possible to take a streetcar across the Oakland Bay Bridge to the Cliff House on the San Francisco waterfront. The immediate area included some shops and amusement rides, but I was fascinated with the ocean. As the name would suggest, the Cliff House stood high on the edge of a cliff, against which big waves crashed constantly. Because this was my first close view of the ocean surf, I enjoyed just sitting while watching and listening as the waves pounded against that part of the shore called Seal Rocks. I took the streetcar to the Cliff House several times during my stay at Camp Knight.

After two weeks as a soldier-carpenter, I was again ordered to prepare for a move. With my belongings packed in my barracks bag, I boarded the ferry and returned with my fellow carpenters to Angel Island. During the next few days, we received inoculations and turned in our heavy-weight uniforms. Apparently, the supply of small sizes of clothing was limited; the fatigues I received were much too large for me. In a letter to my sister I related how I had improved my lot: "I just made a good trade. I swapped a pair of coveralls that were about six inches too long in the arms and legs to a fellow GI for a brand new two-piece fatigue suit that is only about two inches too large."

We exercised each day by hiking around the perimeter of the island; but on the morning of February 7, 1944, instead of hiking, we boarded the ferry that took us back to the Oakland pier. This time, however, we boarded a Victory ship, the *USAT Sea Corporal,* bound for an unknown destination. Our reprieve had ended.

2

Overseas
The Southwest Pacific

As we weighed anchor later that afternoon, the deck was filled with anxious and excited troops. The ship moved slowly and smoothly across the bay, under the Golden Gate Bridge, and out toward the open ocean. We were underway. I wondered about our destination and what the future held in store for us. As I looked back, the city, the bay, and its bridges made a beautiful picture in the late afternoon sun. I had a spot by the starboard rail, there was a cool breeze, and I was enjoying the beginning of my first ocean voyage.

We had traveled only a few miles past the bridge when the ship began to roll and pitch, at first gently, but as time passed, in a more pronounced manner. Soon the deck was much less crowded. The motion of the ship became noticeably more violent, and I began to feel a little light-headed. I decided that it might be wise to visit the head. As I went below, it seemed that the motion of the ship became even more pronounced. I reached the head, went in, and was greeted by a sight that defied description. Seasick GIs, with heads hanging over toilets and urinals, filled the room. The odor was unbearable, at least for me. With all haste I headed for an open space at one of the urinals.

Shortly afterward, sweating and feeling queasy, I headed for my bunk. Unfortunately, the compartment to which I had been assigned was in the bow of the ship. This, of course, exaggerated the upward and downward motion of the ship. I felt as if I were on an elevator. I found my bunk and quickly climbed into it. The bunks were made up of strips of canvas six feet long and two feet wide, laced with rope through grommets to a frame of metal pipes. They were held in place by metal uprights and chains. A space of about two feet separated each bunk from the one above it. It was not possible to sit in an upright position on them. The bunks on the ship were in a five-high configuration, and I had chosen a bottom bunk. That was a mistake, because the four GIs above me had to use the frame of my bunk as a step every time they entered or left their bunks, and on the first few days most of us made frequent trips to the head.

I had been on my bunk for only a short time when a young second lieutenant, troop list in hand, came into our compartment, called out a number of names from the list, and announced that those whose names had been called should report to the galley the following day at 0600 for KP duty. Of course, my name was among those called. I had again been victimized by the alphabetical troop roster. Because I was feeling so sick at that moment, the announcement had little immediate impact on me.

Soon, a voice coming over the compartment loudspeaker demanded our attention with what was to become a familiar "Now hear this." The announcement was that the evening meal was being served, but for most of us, the thought of eating was out of the question. The chow line was very short that first night at sea. I stayed in my bunk listening to the groaning and creaking of the ship until I fell asleep.

When I was awakened by the lieutenant the next morning, I thought that I was feeling a little better; however, as soon as I was on my feet, that queasy feeling returned. I managed to make my way to the galley, where I took my place as server in the chow line. The odor of the food just added to my misery. I made it through the meal and then was encouraged to eat. I was told that it was best to have some food in my stomach. I did not heed that good advice. As soon as the lieutenant was out of sight, I beat a hasty retreat to my bunk.

Shortly before lunch the lieutenant found me, still in my bunk, and ordered me to return to the galley to help with the noon meal. The same sequence of events followed. I served those who came through the chow line, but at the first opportunity, I fled to my bunk. Before I could fall asleep, I saw the lieutenant heading toward me. Prepared for the worst, I started to get up. Apparently I must have been a pitiful sight, because after one look at me the lieutenant said, "Aw, forget it. Go on back to your sack." I never saw that young second lieutenant again, but I still haven't forgotten his kindness to me that afternoon. As I climbed back into my bunk, I recalled the stories my dad had often told about getting seasick when he came to the United States aboard ship. I always laughed as he related how awful he felt. That afternoon, however, I could find nothing the least bit humorous about being seasick.

It was the morning of the fourth day before I felt well enough to eat. I had gone two and a half days without food. I don't know if medication for motion sickness was available in those days, but none was ever offered to me. After eating breakfast, I put on my life preserver, which was called a Mae West, and went up on deck. It was the first time since the afternoon of the first day of the trip that I had breathed the fresh air. It was a beautiful sunny morning. An invigorating breeze was blowing. It seemed that life might be worth living after all. I remember being surprised when I neared the rail and got my first look at the ocean that morning. I could not believe how close the horizon appeared to be. The bright blue ocean seemed to be too small. I never had that feeling again. I'm not sure why.

From that day on, I took every opportunity to stay topside rather than below deck. It seemed to me that there was usually a disagreeable odor in the compartments below deck. I don't know what caused the odor, but it could best be described as stale. I was a much better and happier sailor when I could see the ocean, feel the breeze, and breathe the fresh, clean air. Another thing that I did not like about the ship was that fresh water was available only for drinking. All washbasins and showers delivered saltwater. A special soap formulated for saltwater was supplied, but I never felt really clean after a saltwater shower.

As the days passed, we continued our steady progress toward our unknown destination. We traveled without any escorting warships. The ship followed a zigzag course to make it a more difficult target for enemy planes or subs. Our destination continued to be a well-kept secret; however, I could tell by observing the sun that we were heading in a southwesterly direction. The weather was pleasantly warm, so I spent many hours on deck enjoying the fresh air and watching flying fish and porpoises. It seemed at times that the porpoises were escorting us as they swam alongside. On many evenings after the sun had set, I would lie on deck and watch the stars or stand at the rail to observe the phosphorescent glow of the ocean in the wake of the ship.

On the morning of February 14th, after the familiar "Now hear this," a voice on the speaker system announced that the ship would cross the equator later that day. A ceremony would take place to initiate all those who had not previously made the crossing. That afternoon King Neptune, accompanied by several members of his crew, scrubbed and hosed off three "volunteers," who represented all the soldiers aboard the ship. One of those selected was a man who bragged that he had crossed the equator previously on a cruise ship. Of course, he had no proof of that happening; when he continued to sound off, he was chosen to be one of those reluctant volunteers.

Each of us received a certificate announcing to all mermaids, whales, sea serpents, porpoises, sharks, eels, dolphins, skates, suckers, crabs, lobsters, and all other living things of the sea that we had been initiated into "The Solemn Mysteries of the Ancient Order of the Deep" and had been found worthy to be numbered as trusty shellbacks.

After we had been underway for about ten days, we learned that one member of the ship's crew had been diagnosed as having spinal meningitis. We were cautioned to report to the ship's hospital immediately if we did not feel well, particularly if we felt any stiffness in our necks. The voyage continued without further incident. We never sighted another ship during the entire journey. Other than lifeboat drills, nothing broke up the daily routine until, on the morning of February 23rd, our seventeenth day at sea, land was sighted. We learned that we would dock at Brisbane, Australia, that afternoon. At that time, Brisbane was the site of the headquarters of General Douglas MacArthur, the commander of all Allied troops in the Southwest Pacific Area. The area under MacArthur's command included Australia, New Guinea, Netherlands East Indies, Borneo, and the Philippines.

After the ship docked, we debarked and marched through a section of the city to a racehorse track. We were being quarantined because of the case of meningitis that had been diagnosed aboard ship. Tents were set up in the center of the track, and we were restricted to the area. Our exploration of the land down under was put on hold. Later that evening, I discovered that the date was February 24th. We had lost a day by crossing the international date line before reaching Australia. As I climbed into my bunk that evening, I was happy to be on dry land again.

The next morning I was "treated" to my first breakfast of powdered eggs. The "eggs" were prepared in a field kitchen that had been set up at the track. As I passed through the chow line, a large ladle of a watery greenish-yellow mass was unceremoniously deposited in a compartment of my mess kit. My first taste confirmed my worst fears; the eggs tasted as bad as they looked.

The quarantine was lifted after four days, and we were told to pack our gear and be ready to move out. Shortly afterward, we went by truck to a train station and immediately boarded a train. Our stay in Brisbane was about to end. We had seen almost nothing of the city. The train, which operated on a narrow-gauge track, was small and outdated by U.S. standards. At that time, the Australian rail system was so antiquated that each province had a different track gauge. To go from one province to another, it was necessary to change trains. It was midsummer in Australia, the temperature in the cars was high, and the wooden seats were hard. We had an uncomfortable journey. It was night by the time we reached our destination, Rockhampton, a small town astride the Tropic of Capricorn about 400 miles north of Brisbane. We transferred to trucks for a short ride to an army camp, where we were assigned bunks and went to bed.

The next morning we were told that we had been assigned to the 3rd Battalion of the 162nd Infantry, a regiment of the 41st Infantry Division. We also learned that we were presently in Headquarters Company but that within a few days most of us would be assigned to other companies within the battalion. For me, the wait was only a day or two. I was assigned to Company I, a rifle company. Hoping that this would be my last move for a while, I packed my gear, hoisted my barracks bag, and started down a road to Company I headquarters. I reported to First Sergeant Maurice Kelley and was told that I was being assigned as a rifleman to the second squad of the second platoon. I met my squad leader, Staff Sergeant Del Cochran, who took me under his wing, introduced me to the other squad members, and showed me where I would bed down during the rest of our stay in Rockhampton. Sergeant Cochran, one of the original members of the company, was a wavy-haired blond Oregonian in his mid-20s. He went out of his way to welcome me and to make me feel that I was a valued member of his squad.

During the next two or three weeks, most of my time was spent in getting acquainted with the members of my outfit and learning about the 41st Division. I learned that at the beginning of the war, the division was composed predominately of National Guard units from the Northwestern states of Oregon, Washington, Idaho, and Montana, supplemented by Selective Service inductees. About 70 percent of the troops were members of the National Guard.[1] The 162nd Infantry was composed of units from cities and towns in Oregon. Company I was staffed originally by 129 men from Bend, Oregon, and the nearby area. All of the veteran members of my platoon assured me that Bend, a small town on the eastern slope of the Cascade Mountains, was the prettiest town in the United States. The division was activated on September 16, 1940, fifteen months before the bombing of Pearl Harbor. The original members of the outfit had already served three and a half years when I joined the division in early March 1944.

When war was declared by the U.S. Congress on December 8, 1941, the 41st Division under the command of General Horace Fuller was stationed at Fort Lewis, Washington. The division at that time was composed of four regiments, the 161st, 162nd, 163rd, and 186th. During January 1942, the U.S. Army initiated a program to streamline its infantry divisions by reorganizing its square divisions of four regiments into triangular divisions of three regiments. This was accomplished in the 41st Division by the transfer of the 161st Infantry into the U.S. 25th Division.

After the reorganization, an infantry division, including artillery, support, and supply units, numbered 13,472 enlisted men plus 781 officers. Each of the three regiments was made up of three

1. McCartney, *The Jungleers,* p. 1.

infantry battalions plus an artillery battalion armed with twelve 105-mm howitzers. An artillery battalion with twelve 155-mm howitzers was also assigned to each division.

Those units in the 41st Division were the 146th, 167th, 205th, and the 218th Field Artillery Battalions. Other units in the Division were the 641st Tank Destroyer Battalion armed with 57-mm antitank guns, the 116th Medical Battalion, the 116th Engineer Battalion, the 116th Quartermaster Battalion, the 741st Ordnance Company, the 41st Signal Company, the 41st Reconnaissance Troop, and an MP (military police) platoon.

Each infantry battalion consisted of a heavy-weapons company and three rifle companies. The heavy-weapons company was equipped with 81-mm mortars and .30-caliber water-cooled machine guns. Rifle companies were made up of three rifle platoons and a weapons platoon. Rifle platoons had three twelve-man squads. In addition to the squad leader and his assistant, each squad was made up of two scouts, a BAR team, and five riflemen. The first scout was usually armed with a tommy gun (Thompson submachine gun), a .45-caliber automatic weapon with a twenty-round magazine. The three-man BAR team was armed with a BAR and two carbines. The team members took turns carrying the BAR and the ammunition for it. All other squad members carried M1 Garands. Each platoon had a three-man bazooka team. The firepower of the weapons platoon was supplied by three 60-mm mortars and two .30-caliber air-cooled machine guns. When the company went into combat, one medic was usually assigned to each platoon.

A rifle company at full strength numbered 182 enlisted men plus six officers: the CO, an executive officer, and four platoon leaders. A runner was assigned to each officer. Squad leaders and assistant squad leaders were noncoms, as were most of the members of company headquarters. The top sergeant, supply sergeant, mess sergeant, company clerk, armorer, and cooks were all members of the company headquarters.

Late in February 1942, the 162nd Infantry moved by train from Fort Lewis to Fort Dix, New Jersey, where the men boarded ships in early March. After an arduous voyage of forty days, the troops debarked at Melbourne, Australia, on April 10th. The 163rd Infantry had arrived at Sydney four days earlier and was en route to Mel-

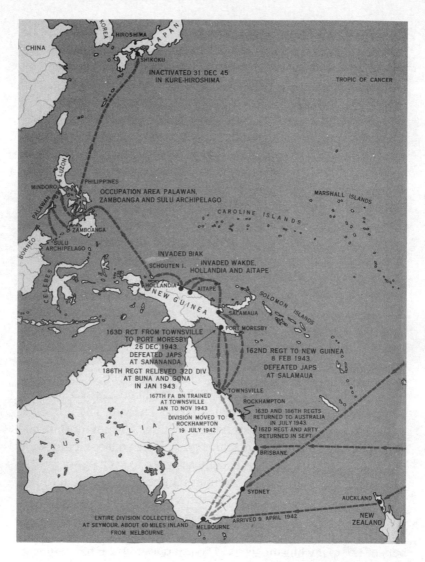

Route of the 41st Infantry Division in World War II. From McCartney, *The Jungleers.*

bourne when the 162nd Infantry arrived. By May 13th, all of the division had landed in Australia. The 41st Division was the first U.S. division to be sent overseas in World War II. The 41st Division and the 32nd Division, which arrived in Australia shortly after the 41st, were the first U.S. divisions to come under the command of General Douglas MacArthur, who had arrived in Australia about a month earlier.[2]

The U.S. troops arrived at a time when the Japanese army was advancing down the eastern coast of New Guinea to threaten Australia. The Aussies, I was told, were overjoyed to see our troops because most of the Australian army was either in North Africa fighting the German army or in New Guinea trying to stop the advance of the Japanese, who were attempting to reach Port Moresby by crossing the Owen Stanley Mountains along the Kokoda Trail.

The 41st Division set up camp at Seymour and began training exercises. During July, the division moved north to Rockhampton and started training for amphibious landings and jungle warfare. Late in December, the 163rd Infantry boarded ships that carried the regiment to Port Moresby, New Guinea, arriving on December 27, 1942. Within a few days, the regiment was flown north to Dobodura and made a one-day march to relieve an Australian battalion that was positioned to attack the Japanese at Sanananda Point. During three weeks of hard fighting, the men of the 163rd Infantry, in their baptism of fire, killed 1,400 Japanese and cleared Sanananda Point.

Late in the month of January 1943, the 186th Infantry was flown to New Guinea to relieve units of the U.S. 32nd Division at Buna and Gona. The role of the 186th Infantry was to patrol and mop up any Japanese still in the vicinity.

On February 8, 1943, the 162nd Infantry boarded ships that sailed across the Coral Sea to Port Moresby. The regiment moved to Milne Bay and during the next four months moved to Buna, then to Gona, and finally to the Sanananda area, where they relieved units of the 163rd Infantry. During the night of June 29th, the 1st Battalion of the 162nd Infantry made an unopposed amphibious landing at Nassau Bay, about ten miles south of Salamaua. By July 6th, the remainder of the regiment had landed at Nassau Bay and,

---

2. McCartney, *The Jungleers*, pp. 19, 21–22, 26.

in conjunction with Australian forces, prepared to move north to Salamaua. After seventy-six consecutive days of combat, a record for continuous contact with an enemy, Salamaua fell to the battle-weary troops of the 162nd Infantry. During the battle 1,272 Japanese were killed at the cost of eighty-nine U.S. lives. The 41st Division had been "blooded," a term used by the army to describe a unit that had taken part in its first combat.[3]

By early October 1943, the division had returned to Australia, where a rest camp was set up at Rockhampton. The men were granted short furloughs, and the process of bringing the division back to full strength with replacements and returning veterans began. I was one of those replacements. Many of the original members of our platoon did not return. When the platoon reached full strength shortly after my arrival, about two-thirds of its members were replacements.

The camp at Rockhampton was made up of tents pitched among trees on the outskirts of town. Each tent held six canvas army cots furnished with mosquito netting that hung from wooden racks built over the bunks. I occupied a tent with five squad members. As the days passed, I listened to countless stories related by the veterans of the Salamaua campaign about the hardships they endured during the long battle. There were numerous stories about the battles for Roosevelt Ridge and Scout Ridge, but there was little, if any, recounting of individual exploits. The emphasis was on the accomplishments of the company, the battalion, and the regiment. It was evident that I had joined an outfit with a lot of pride in its combat record.

Most of my memories about Australia are centered on Rockhampton, a small town of 35,000 in Queensland Province. I remember strolling the streets of the town, stopping at milk bars, where I had my first taste of ice cream since leaving the United States. Everything seemed to be twenty years behind the times. The cars were small and had right-hand drive, the streets were narrow, and the pace was slow. The money system was strange to me. I was not in Australia long enough to become comfortable with the relative values of pounds, shillings, quids, and pence. When I

3. McCartney, The Jungleers, pp. 33, 41–44, 51, 70.

made a purchase, I would pay with a big bill and wait, trusting that I would receive the correct change.

I enjoyed listening to the Aussies; it seemed that everything was either "bloomin'" or "bloody." Everyone was a "mate" to the Australians. "Styke and eyegs" (steak and eggs) was a favorite meal. If you were "knocked up," it meant that you were worn out or just tired.

I remember a trip to the movies one warm evening. Rockhampton was in a semi-tropical climate zone, and the movie theater was outdoors in a coconut grove. Each row of seats was constructed with two long coconut logs, one mounted at knee level, the other at shoulder height. Each seat was formed by attaching a strip of canvas about two feet wide to the logs to make a seat similar to a lawn chair. It was an unusual but attractive setting for a theater. I don't remember the name of the movie, but I do recall that Nelson Eddy and Jeanette McDonald were the stars.

My stay in Rockhampton was short, only about three weeks, and the training exercises were relatively few and easy. Rumors of an impending move to New Guinea were widely circulated, and everyone expected that the 41st Division would soon be back in action. One afternoon we were gathered for a training lecture given by our platoon leader, a recent replacement in the company. The young lieutenant, whom we called a ninety-day wonder because OCS lasted only ninety days, talked to us about the days ahead. He acknowledged that combat was in the near future. He went on to tell us what he expected of us when those days came to pass. The important thing, he said, was not whether we were wounded or killed, but that we gain our objectives. If there was a hill to be taken, we would take it even if it cost most of us our lives.

I pictured us being mowed down by machine-gun fire from pillboxes as we charged up a hill. That image certainly did not appeal to me. Apparently it did not sit well with our platoon sergeant, Les Perry, either, because after the lieutenant left, he did not immediately dismiss us as our platoon leader had ordered. Sergeant Perry, a combat veteran, waited until the lieutenant was out of sight. Then he told us not to worry too much about what the lieutenant had said. We would take our objectives, but we would not take them in the foolhardy manner described by our leader. The sergeant closed by saying that he expected to be alive and to return to his home in Bend after the war. I went back to my tent feeling a lot better.

In mid-March 1944, the order came down to break camp and move out. We went by truck to Gladstone, a town on the east coast near Rockhampton, where we immediately boarded a ship that was to take us to New Guinea. At least, that was what everyone expected. As we reached the top of the gangplank a sailor awaited us beside a stack of large plywood sheets. He handed each of us a sheet off the stack. The plywood, we were told, was to be used as a bunk during the voyage.

We quickly discovered that we were on a cargo ship, not a troop transport. A tent was set up on the top deck to serve as a kitchen. Australian mutton was hanging in the open air, and boxes of canned food and sacks of potatoes were stacked on the deck. Temporary toilets constructed of wood were positioned on the fantail of the ship. Drinking water, we learned, would be available for an hour each morning and afternoon. We could fill our canteens at that time. It seemed that this would not be one of those luxury cruises. However, the price was right; all expenses were paid by Uncle Sam.

The first order of business was to find a place for my "bed." I decided on a spot in a hold near an open stairway. I thought that I would get some fresh air at that location. After stowing my barracks bag on my "bunk," I returned to the open deck to watch our departure from the land down under. After the evening meal, I stayed topside enjoying the warm breeze. When darkness fell, I watched the stars until I was ready to hit the sack. I went below deck and stretched out on my bunk. The plywood was hard but smooth and certainly made a better bed than the cold steel deck. I quickly fell asleep but was awakened at some point during the night by several large sacks of potatoes falling down the open steps and landing dangerously close to me. The potatoes had been dislodged when the ship encountered the rough water of the Coral Sea. I decided immediately to change the location of my bunk. With my sheet of plywood in hand, I climbed the stairs and found an open spot on the deck above. I slept under the stars during the rest of the trip.

The next morning I found that we had joined a convoy of six or seven ships. The convoy moved slowly, the speed being dictated by the slowest ship. The direction of our movement was to the north.

Nothing of consequence happened until land was sighted after we had been en route for about a week. We anchored in a harbor with the most beautiful clear blue water I had ever seen. We tossed coins into the water and watched them for an incredibly long time as they sank to the bottom of the bay. We learned that we were anchored in Milne Bay at the extreme southeastern point of Papua New Guinea. At that time, New Guinea, whose shape resembled that of a guinea hen, was divided into three sections. The western half, Dutch New Guinea, was ruled by the Netherlands. Papua and Northeast New Guinea were lumped together and were governed by the Australia New Guinea Administrative Unit.

We did not linger long at Milne Bay; the next morning we resumed our voyage to the north. The waters were becoming increasingly dangerous, so the convoy traveled within sight of the shoreline during the remainder of the trip. Three or four days later, we arrived at our destination, Finschhafen, a town on the eastern coast of New Guinea that had been recently wrested from the Japanese by the Aussies.

As I set foot on New Guinea for the first time, I could feel the intense heat and oppressive humidity of the jungle. There was also a stale, musty odor that was foreign to me. Mud was everywhere. We slogged through the muck and climbed aboard trucks that were to take us to a bivouac area at Cape Cretin. As the trucks made their way up the crude road through the jungle, a feeling of apprehension came over me.

For the next few days, we were busy setting up a tent camp. We received supplies and clothing as we prepared for the days ahead. A small group of new replacements joined the company at that time. It was then the first week in April and I had not received any mail since leaving the United States on February 6th. Late in the week, however, I did receive a letter from my sister Margaret that had been written on March 17th. Of course I was happy to receive the letter, but I knew that someone in my family wrote to me almost every day, and I wondered what had happened to all the letters written during the six weeks preceding St. Patrick's Day. I was reminded by reading the letter that my twentieth birthday, March 16th, had passed almost unnoticed while I was at Rockhampton. I was no longer a teenager.

Later that afternoon we learned that the next day, Easter Sunday, would be a holiday. I attended Mass and received Holy Communion on Easter. There was no chapel, so the priest set up a portable altar in a tent; there were a lot of GIs in attendance. We prayed to the Lord for His protection during the combat that would soon be at hand. It was the first Mass I had attended since leaving the United States. After Mass, I wrote to my mother, "Last Easter Sunday I was at Sportsman's Park watching the Browns beat the Cardinals. Things can certainly change in a year."

During the next week or so, speculation about the location of the next action continued. Most of the veterans predicted that Wewak, on the northern coast of New Guinea, would be our target. In the early months of the war, the Japanese had occupied strategic spots along the coast of New Guinea, the second largest island in the world. The Japs had progressed to a point only thirty-two miles north of Port Moresby on the southern coast before being stopped by the Australians in September 1942. Since that time, the U.S. 32nd and 41st Divisions along with the Aussies had moved up the coast, systematically taking the closest Japanese position to the north. If that pattern was followed, the next landing would be at Wewak.

In mid-April, each of us was given a list of items to be carried during an upcoming practice landing. The list given to me read as follows:

M1 rifle	spoon
bayonet and scabbard	canteen
.30-caliber ammo—12 clips of 8 rounds each	canteen cup
	canteen cover
hand grenades—four	K-rations—six boxes
60-mm mortar shell	toothbrush
gas mask	toothpaste
pack	razor
entrenching tool—pick	shave cream
first aid kit	matches
insect repellant	steel helmet
Atabrine	helmet liner
water purification pills	fatigue cap
life preservers (inflatable)—two	ammunition belt

poncho	extra socks—one pair
mess kit	extra underwear—one pair
knife	extra handkerchief—one
fork	

I dutifully gathered every item on the list and was in the process of loading my pack when one of the veterans, Hubert Baxley, with whom I shared our tent, saw what I was doing and said, "You'll never be able to make it through the jungle carrying a load like that." He suggested several things to leave behind, but I was leery about not following orders, so I continued to load everything listed into my pack.

The next morning, we climbed aboard trucks that took us to the coast. There we boarded an LCI (landing craft, infantry). The LCI, which was 157 feet long and 23 feet wide, was designed to carry an infantry company plus the ship's crew. It did not have a flat bottom like most landing craft. It was designed so that it could be beached, whereupon two long ramps, one on either side of the bow of the ship, would be lowered to allow the troops to debark.

Shortly after boarding, we set out to sea for our dress rehearsal. We were told that we would go a short distance down the coast and land near the town of Lae. As I stood on deck I could see ships all around us. I was surprised and impressed by the size of the convoy. As we approached our objective, we were ordered to go to our compartments below deck, where we were given instructions for the landing. We were told that when we made the real landing, it was likely that we would be under enemy fire, so it was important to get off the landing craft as quickly as possible. We were instructed to remain in our compartments until the ship had beached, and then to go up the stairs, across the deck, and down the closest ramp as quickly as possible.

As we approached the beach that day, the time before landing was counted off over the ship's speakers. One minute, thirty seconds, ten seconds, five seconds, and we hit the beach with a jolt. Following the man in front of me, I sped up the steps, across the deck, and down the port ramp. The ramp was steep, and I picked up speed as I descended. When I hit the beach, which was sloping up almost as steeply as the ramp was sloping down, my legs would not hold me; I fell forward, driving the barrel of my rifle into the sand. I got

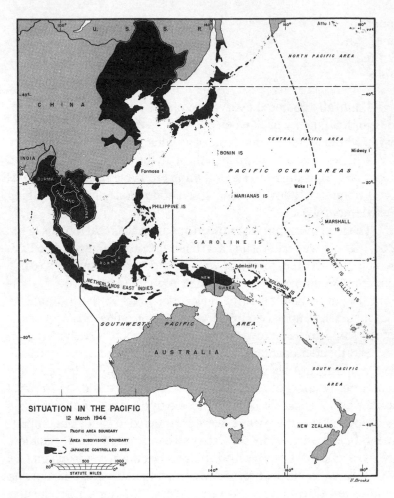

Situation in the Pacific, March 12, 1944. From Smith, *The Approach to the Philippines.*

up quickly, hoping not too many people had seen me fall. It was fortunate that this had not been the actual assault. My rifle was in no condition to do battle with the Nips; the barrel was loaded with sand. When I got back to my tent that night, I asked Hugh for advice. He promised to help when the time for the real thing was at hand.

Several days later, we attended a briefing about the upcoming action. We entered a large tent, where a huge topographic model of a coastline and surrounding area stood on supports about the height of a table top. We saw before us a layout of our next objectives, the town and airdromes of Hollandia in Dutch New Guinea, about 600 miles west of our present location at Finschhafen.

All the rumors had been wrong; Wewak would be bypassed. We were told that numerous efforts had been made to convince the Japs that Wewak would be our next objective. Empty life rafts had been floated ashore, dummy parachutes had been dropped, and the area had been subjected to naval and air bombardments. Hopefully the Japanese would swallow the bait.

We learned that the attacking forces would include two divisions, the 24th Division, commanded by General Frederick Irving, and our 41st Division. Two regiments of the 41st Division, the 162nd and the 186th, would land at Humboldt Bay near the town of Hollandia. The 24th Division would land at Depapre, twenty-five miles northwest of Hollandia; the 41st Division's 163rd Infantry would land at Aitape, 123 miles east of Hollandia. The landings near Hollandia were designated as Operation RECKLESS; the landing at Aitape carried the code name Operation PERSECUTION. General Robert Eichelberger was designated as commander of the RECKLESS Task Force. General Jens Doe, the commander of the 163rd Infantry, would be in command of the PERSECUTION forces.[4] Because the U.S. air base nearest Hollandia was at Nadzab, about 500 miles southeast, the objective of the Aitape landing was to capture lightly held airstrips closer to Hollandia. It was expected that those airstrips could almost immediately be used by fighter planes to provide land-based air support for the Hollandia operation. The attack plan at Hollandia called for the 24th Division and the remaining two regiments of the 41st to form a pincers, or double-envelopment movement, around the 7,000-ft. Cyclops Mountains to capture the airfields about fifteen miles inland from the landing beaches.

H-hour was planned for 0700, the hour of high tide, on April 22, 1944. The 3rd Battalion 162nd Infantry would provide the assault troops at Humboldt Bay. Companies K and L would land at H-hour; Company I at H plus 15. Our landing site was designated as White Beach 1. The location of the beach was pointed out on the

---

4. Smith, *The Approach to the Philippines,* pp. 29–30.

topographic model. Our first objective, Pancake Hill, was also pin-pointed. It was described to us as a treeless, flat-topped hill over-looking the landing beach. The major objective of our battalion was the town of Hollandia, about two and a half miles as the crow flies from the landing beach. I was impressed by the detail of the planning. I was also impressed by the size and detail of the topo-graphic model. It was not something I ever expected to see in such a primitive area. It was also the only one that I ever saw.

That night I sought the help of my veteran buddy as we pre-pared our packs. We were to board an LCI the next afternoon. One item had been removed from the original list—the 60-mm mortar shell. The mortar shells were normally carried by members of the weapons platoon. I was happy to be relieved of that burden. The grenades issued to us were Australian grenades. They were some-what larger and heavier than U.S. grenades, which weighed about a pound and a half. Hugh said that he preferred the Aussie gre-nades to ours because they were more powerful than U.S. grenades and showed a less visible trail of light when thrown at night. He warned me that the Aussie grenades had a four-second fuse, one second shorter than U.S. grenades.

We went down the required list of items and eliminated the mess kit, table knife, and undershirts. Hugh said that we would live on K-rations; there would be no need for a mess kit or knife. We would eat out of cans with a spoon or fork. Then we opened the six boxes of K-rations and discarded the boxes. I gave my cigarettes to a squad member who smoked. I left behind half of the hardtack biscuits and put the remaining rations into two small rubber bags. At the suggestion of the veteran, I put a long-sleeved sweatshirt, several V-mail forms, and a pencil into my pack. Hugh said that often we would be soaking wet from the numerous rains; the dry sweatshirt would be a luxury in the foxhole at night. The writing supplies would be used to write letters to my family and friends. Hugh also said that we would be checked to be sure we had gas masks when we boarded the LCI. He suggested that I could toss my mask overboard on the night before D-Day. Hugh's final sug-gestion was that if I planned to carry any items that I didn't want to get wet, such as my wallet or any pictures, I should put them above the support straps in my helmet liner.

3

Hollandia
The RECKLESS Task Force

The next morning, April 19th, the members of our company boarded an LCI, stowed our gear in the compartments below deck, and anxiously awaited our departure. It was early evening before we were underway. Rather than taking a direct westerly route toward Hollandia, the convoy headed due north, past the western tip of New Britain.

When I went on deck the next morning, I was greeted by the sight of ships in every direction as far as the eye could see. The ships were of every size and description imaginable. There were LCIs, LSTs (landing ships, tank) and LSDs (landing ships, dock). Smaller landing craft such as LCTs (landing craft, tank), LCMs (landing craft, mechanized), LVTs (landing vehicles, tracked), and LCVPs (landing craft, vehicle and personnel) were carried aboard the larger ships. There were troop transports, cargo ships, mine sweepers, and warships in the convoy. Destroyers, cruisers, and aircraft carriers assured that the convoy would have adequate protection. The sight of such a powerful force gave me a feeling of confidence about the outcome of the upcoming landing.

Later that afternoon, we landed on Manus Island in the Admiralties. The island had recently been taken by the 1st Cavalry Division. Mopping up was still in progress. We were allowed to debark and stretch our legs. We went ashore and slogged through the mud in a grove of coconut trees. Many of the trees had been knocked down or had their tops broken off by the pre-landing naval and air bombardments. During the few hours of our layover in Seeadler Harbor, more warships joined the convoy, increasing its size to 217 ships.[1] It was by far the largest attack force of the war in the Southwest Pacific to that time.

The convoy, under the command of Admiral Daniel Barbey, was carrying 84,000 troops, including 50,000 combat troops, to the three landing beaches. The convoy included eight aircraft carriers with their screen of seventeen destroyers.[2] General MacArthur had requested that the carriers remain at Hollandia until D-Day plus eight; but Admiral Chester Nimitz, commander of the Pacific Fleet, felt that it would be too dangerous and agreed to keep the carriers there only through D-Day plus three. At that time the carriers would withdraw to rejoin the fleet. Admiral Barbey would remain in charge of operations until the landing force commanders had established headquarters ashore.[3]

We were back en route before dark, again heading north to deceive the Japanese. Under cover of darkness, our course would change to take us toward Hollandia. That night and the following day passed without incident as the huge convoy sailed on a westerly course.

On the evening of April 21st, I was informed that I would stand watch that night on a 20-mm anti-aircraft gun. Before I could protest that I knew nothing about anti-aircraft guns, I was told to follow a sailor up a flight of stairs to the top of the conning tower, the highest point on the landing craft, where the gun was mounted. The sailor told me that all I needed to do was sit in the chair by the gun and watch for any planes. If I were to see a plane, I should press a button to sound an alarm, then point the gun at the plane. By that time, a member of the ship's crew would be there to take over.

I was awakened by a sailor during the night to stand watch. I climbed the steps to the top of the tower and watched the starry sky, all the while wondering what awaited us on White Beach 1 the next morning. The night was warm and the stars were beautiful. My one-

1. Drea, *MacArthur's ULTRA*, p. 105.
2. Smith, *The Approach to the Philippines*, pp. 29–31.
3. Morison, *New Guinea and the Marianas*, pp. 68–69.

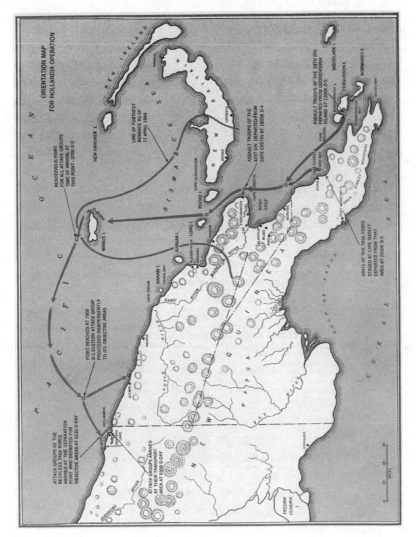

Orientation map for Hollandia operation. From McCartney, *The Jungleers*.

hour watch passed; I saw no planes. I was relieved by the GI who had the next watch, went below to my compartment, climbed into my bunk, said a short prayer, and fell asleep.

During the night, the convoy split. The PERSECUTION Task Force, with Captain Alfred Noble in charge, headed for Aitape. The RECKLESS Task Force also split. With Admiral Barbey in command, the NOISELESS Task Force carrying the 24th Division set course for Tanahmerah Bay. With Admiral William Fechteler in charge, the LETTERPRESS Task Force carrying the 41st Division less the 163rd Infantry continued on course to Humboldt Bay.

It was still very dark when we were awakened the next morning. We had sandwiches and coffee for breakfast. I did not feel like eating, but I forced myself to eat a sandwich anyway. The bombardment was scheduled to begin at 0600, sixty minutes before H-hour. Almost everyone was on deck looking intently at the shoreline of Humboldt Bay as darkness gradually lifted. The sky was overcast and an intermittent drizzle was falling. There was an eerie silence; no one had anything to say. We stood, thinking our own thoughts, until the quiet was broken by the opening salvo from the warships.

Our LCI was positioned with its starboard side overlooking the landing beaches, and everyone rushed to that rail to get the best view as the shells exploded on the beaches. The LCI began to list to that side, and the captain's voice came over the speaker system ordering us to move away from the rail. By this time the noise was deafening, but reassuring. No Japanese planes appeared; all seemed to be going well. The bombardment continued with six destroyers and two rocket LCIs moving close to shore to shell their targets while three cruisers fired from a longer range. Smoke and haze started to build up over the shoreline. LCI rocket ships fired on Pancake Hill, trying to knock out anti-aircraft guns positioned there, while two minesweepers searched in vain for mines in the harbor. [4]

Finally, the carrier-based fighters and bombers joined in, dive-bombing and strafing their targets. Navy Avengers dropped anti-personnel and anti-mine bombs near the beach. They seemed to dive almost into the jungle before rising again. It was a spectacular and unforgettable sight. But now our time neared. We were ordered

4. Morison, *New Guinea and the Marianas*, pp. 69, 82.

below deck to strap on our gear and prepare for the landing. I thought about my misadventure at the practice landing, but I knew what to expect this time and I had a somewhat lighter load. The only things in my pockets were my rosary and a handkerchief. My wallet and photos were in my helmet liner. My dog tags, on which my name, serial number, blood type, and religion were stamped, hung on a chain around my neck. I wore a waterproof watch on my left wrist and carried my ammo in two bandoliers across my chest. Everything else but my rifle was in my pack or attached to my ammo belt. I had thrown my gas mask overboard the previous night to complete my preparation for my first assault landing.

We waited in silence as the time until landing was counted off. The LCI hit the beach with a shudder and we were off, up the steps, across the deck, and down the ramps. The LCI had reached the sandy beach, and the bottoms of the ramps were on dry sand. We did not even get our feet wet as we landed. Companies K and L had preceded us ashore, and we could see GIs to our right on the beach. There was gunfire, but I decided that it was not aimed at us because the veterans seemed unconcerned. The carrier planes were still strafing and bombing the jungle ahead of us. The smoke drifting over the beach carried the odor of the explosives fired during the bombardment.

Our company quickly formed ranks, and we moved out in single file with the first platoon in the lead. As we advanced, we tried to keep a space of about ten to fifteen feet between each man to mini- mize casualties if we were to come under fire. As we moved along the beach toward our first objective, Pancake Hill, about half a mile distant, my feelings were more of excitement than fear. We reached the hill and found anti-aircraft guns but no enemy soldiers. Appar- ently, the Japs had fled into the jungle to escape the heavy shelling of the bombardment that preceded the landing. The hill was secured, and our company moved out through the jungle toward the town of Hollandia as General MacArthur, who came ashore on White Beach 1 later that morning, watched from the deck of the cruiser *Nashville*.[5]

During the early afternoon, our 2nd Platoon replaced the 1st Platoon as the spearhead of the column. It was normal procedure to rotate companies, platoons, and squads so that the danger and stress

5. Morison, *New Guinea and the Marianas*, p. 83.

involved in leading the column could be spread as evenly as possible. It was also normal procedure for the column to be led by two scouts, but on this afternoon our young lieutenant, taking part in his first day of combat, moved out as the leader of the column. It immediately became apparent that the speed of advance had quickened appreciably. It was also evident that we were headed for higher ground above the coast. We were climbing a steep native track through thick brush on a very hot afternoon. It was not easy going.

As we advanced, the trail became even steeper. The weapons platoon was following the three rifle platoons. Marching at the end of a column was always more difficult than marching at the head of a column because the pace was always more uneven or erratic at the rear. Also, the members of the weapons platoon had the added burden of carrying their heavy load of machine guns, mortars, and the ammunition for those weapons. They were having a tough time trying to keep up with the pace being set by the lieutenant.

The normal way to communicate in a column was by passing a message from man to man. As we moved along that afternoon a message was passed to me from the rear, "Tell that damn fool lieutenant to slow down." I passed the message verbatim. I doubt that those exact words reached the lieutenant, but whatever message reached the front did not seem to have much effect on the pace of our advance. We continued to move rapidly up the hill.

As evening approached, we had progressed about two and a half miles from White Beach 1 to a position high on Jarremoh Hill, where we set up a perimeter for the night. The hill, at an elevation of 1,000 feet, overlooked Challenger Cove and the town of Hollandia. Each evening the company commander chose the location of the perimeter. Then each platoon leader would designate foxhole positions for members of his platoon. Working with their fellow platoon leaders, the officers would position the holes to form a circle, an oval, or some configuration that would result in a connected pattern. The holes were usually spaced fifteen to twenty feet apart and were dug large enough to allow two men to sleep while a third sat in the hole on guard duty. The depth of the holes varied depending upon the hardness of the soil or rock, the strength and perseverance of the diggers, and the probability of a night attack or shelling by the enemy. The holes for machine-gun and BAR teams were usually situated at points that would give them good fields of fire if an enemy attack took place. Officers and their runners, the first sergeant, the platoon sergeants, the medics, and some members of company headquarters occupied holes in the center of the perimeter.

The SOP (standard operating procedure) for nights was that everyone would be in his hole from dusk until daylight. No one in the outer perimeter left his hole for any reason whatsoever. We never used a password; there was no need for one. Anything moving outside the perimeter was considered to be the enemy. One man was always on guard in each hole throughout the night. Each watch lasted for one hour, which meant that every man in the outer perimeter would be on guard for three one-hour periods every night. Those who were able to get to sleep immediately would have two hours of sleep between each watch. Company members who slept in the inner perimeter, envied by those in the outer perimeter, were not required to stand watch.

On that first night I shared a foxhole with my squad leader, Del Cochran, and another man whose identity I do not recall. After we finished digging our hole, we put one of our ponchos on the ground and then snapped the other two together. We drove a forked stake into the ground at each end of the hole and placed a third stick between the forked stakes. Then we put the ponchos over the top to form a small tent with openings toward the outside and inside of the perimeter. After a supper of K-rations, I was almost ready for my first night in a foxhole. My fatigues were still wet from a late afternoon rain, so I took my sweatshirt out of my pack and replaced my wet fatigue jacket with the dry sweatshirt. I took out one of my life preservers, which would be my pillow, and inflated it. I said a short prayer and quickly fell asleep.

I was awakened two hours later to serve my watch. With my rifle in my hands and hand grenades at my side, I peered into the blackness. It was so dark that I could not distinguish any forms. The tree canopy blacked out the sky; I couldn't see anything. I decided that I would have to rely on my ears to detect any Nips who might be moving about on that night. I soon learned that there were always night sounds in the jungle—animals, insects, birds, the wind in the trees, rain—any of which could cause a person's imagination to picture a Jap crawling through the jungle. I had been cautioned not to fire my rifle or throw grenades unless I was certain that the Japs were near. I was warned that either action would pinpoint my position for anyone within sight. My hour passed slowly but without incident other than the roar of artillery shells being fired over our heads at the townsite of Hollandia by our artillery and naval guns. At the end of my watch, I woke my squad leader, who was next on watch. I then quickly went back to sleep.

When I was awakened for my second watch, I found that my head was on the hard ground; my pillow was leaking. My watch passed without incident, and after waking Sergeant Cochran, I blew up my pillow and fell asleep.

When it was time for my last watch of the night, I had the impression that it was not quite as dark as it had been earlier. I sat up to take over the watch and to my dismay noticed that I could see my white, long-sleeved sweatshirt. Instead of putting my fatigue jacket over my sweatshirt, I had hung it on a tree out of reach of the hole. I remembered having seen a war movie that showed Japanese snipers hidden in trees shooting our GIs. I immediately decided that if any Japs climbed the trees around us during the night, my white sweatshirt would be the first thing they would see, and I would become their first target. The longer I thought about the situation, the more certain I became that there were Japs in those trees. Mercifully, dawn began to creep across the sky; soon it was daylight. I had survived my first night in a foxhole. I never again wore that sweatshirt without the fatigue jacket over it.

Shortly after daylight, we were on our way toward our objective, the town of Hollandia. We advanced without opposition and soon came to the edge of a clearing where we could see the town. It was a small village of thatched-roof huts scattered in a clearing near the shoreline of Challenger Cove. It appeared to be deserted. There was not a single person—Japanese or native—in sight. We advanced carefully and made a search of the huts. It was obvious that all the native huts had been occupied by the Japanese. There were Japanese books, pictures, utensils, and musical instruments. We even found cosmetics and women's clothing in some of the huts. The capture of the town became a souvenir hunt. I picked up some coins, a pair of ivory chopsticks, an opium pipe, a bayonet, a mandolin, a small bamboo flute, and a stack of invasion money. I took the mandolin because

I could play a violin; and since the mandolin was strung the same as the violin, I knew that I would be able to pick out a few tunes on it.

I assumed that because we had taken our objectives, we would set up camp nearby, but shortly afterward we set out to reach the opposite shore of the cove. Instead of going around the shoreline, we went across the cove. With my rifle over one shoulder and the mandolin over the other, I waded into the waist-high water. The distance across the cove was about half a mile. We had been underway for only a few minutes when a man a short distance ahead of me stepped into a hole and fell into the water. The GI immediately behind him was a big man who reached down, grabbed the collar of the fallen man's fatigue shirt with one hand, and easily pulled him to his feet. We reached the opposite shore without further incident. After a short rest, we were told that we still had to go farther up the shoreline to reach our destination for the night. I decided that the mandolin would go no farther and threw it into the jungle.

We followed a trail along the shore for about two hours. Then we set up our perimeter, ate our K-rations, and settled in for the night. During my first watch, I heard a series of loud explosions coming from the direction of White Beach 1. The next morning, we learned that an enemy bomber had dropped a bomb that had hit an ammunition dump on the beach. Because the beach was very shallow, supplies and ammunition were stacked closely. The explosion had ignited a gasoline dump, and the resulting fire was still burning. Over 60 percent of the ammunition and rations on the beach had been destroyed. Twenty-four men were killed and 100 hurt by the explosion and resulting fire.[6] Until further notice, we were told, we would be on one-third rations: one box of K-rations per day.

I learned from my research for this book that there were two planes involved in the bombing raid. Japanese records indicated that the planes had taken off from Biak, an island 350 miles west of Hollandia.[7] The loss of life and the destruction of supplies were merely a foretaste of the problems we were to encounter later at Biak.

Throughout the war, whenever we were in combat, we lived almost exclusively on K-rations. My memories of K-rations are not

6. Smith, *The Approach to the Philippines*, p. 79.
7. Drea, *MacArthur's ULTRA*, p. 119.

fond ones. The rations were packaged in small waxed paperboard boxes measuring approximately 8 x 3 x 2 inches, about the size of the old Cracker Jack box. Boxes were labeled either breakfast, lunch, or dinner, each containing the "appropriate" meal.

Each box contained two packets of hardtack biscuits, four cigarettes, and a drink packet. The "entree" for each meal was packed in a small can about three inches in diameter and about an inch and a half high. For breakfast, the can contained something called ham and eggs, for lunch an orange-colored cheese, and for dinner a concoction called corned pork and apple flakes. We used miniature folding can openers to open the ration cans. Those openers were very effective and easy to use, even though they measured only five-eighths by one and a half inches when folded. I still have one of those openers and have used it on several occasions over the past fifty years. The breakfast box contained a packet of instant coffee, a small dried fruit bar, matches, and a small pack of toilet paper. For lunch there was a melt-proof chocolate bar and powdered lemonade. The dinner box contained a few pieces of hard candy, instant coffee, and a bouillon cube, which we seldom used. The only variation occurred when the rations were packed in Australia. When that was the case, the drink for every meal was tea.

Most of the time the meals were eaten cold. We seldom built large fires for fear of disclosing our position. Those men who liked coffee did make small fires by burning the waxed paperboard ration boxes. Drinking water was almost always in short supply, and a lunch of hardtack biscuits and dry cheese with a few swallows of water was definitely not a gourmet meal. One man suggested that the hardtack be eaten only to ward off imminent starvation. The best meal was breakfast. The "ham and eggs" were reasonably tasty, even cold. The dinner of pork and apple flakes was edible at best. The hard candy was good, the fruit bar was acceptable, but the "chocolate" bar left much to be desired.

Beginning the morning of the third day, the major mission of our company was to secure the position we had occupied on the shore of the bay north of Hollandia and to send out patrols in search of any Japs who might be in the surrounding area. Because of the food shortage, all patrols were ordered to look for Japanese rations in and around all buildings. The worst of the ration emergency lasted about one week. During that time, we were able to find a few bags of rice and some canned salmon that helped get us through the crisis. The situation gradually improved, but we were not supplied with full rations until May 15th.

In addition to the shortage of food, there was another problem that affected many of the men in our outfit—a shortage of cigarettes. With the exception of a few Japanese cigarettes we found in buildings, K-rations were the only source of cigarettes. Most of the smokers really suffered when their supply of cigarettes ran out. I learned what a strong addiction tobacco could be when I watched a few men smoking at night in foxholes with ponchos covering their heads. I hated to see that happen. I felt that those men were risking their lives and the lives of all their buddies. I decided then that I would never become a smoker.

Early one morning, a squad left on a patrol; we expected them back by early or mid-afternoon. The day went on and there was no sign of the patrol. Concern for their safety began to grow until late afternoon, when from somewhere in the distance, voices could be heard. As the voices grew louder it began to sound somewhat like singing. Soon the tardy patrol came into view, and it became obvious that most of the men were drunk. After they reached our perimeter, some of the men collapsed onto the ground. One man who was still in reasonably good shape related the story of the misadventures of the patrol.

The men discovered a cave, and upon entering found, among other things, a case of Japanese sake. They sat in the relatively cool cave and enjoyed their find. When they decided that it was time to start back and came out into the hot midday sun, some of the men could not walk without help. The march back was a slow and staggering one. I don't know if the men were disciplined or if the CO, Captain Eulon Richardson, felt that they had suffered enough. I do know that several of the men were still hurting the next morning and throughout most of the day. I can still picture one of the men lying on his back with his mouth half open while flies walked on his face. He was too sick to even brush the flies away.

It was very fortunate for me that we were able to maintain our perimeter at the same location for about two weeks because I had picked up a bad case of "jungle rot" during the few days since our landing. I don't know what the proper medical diagnosis would be, but the condition could best be described as large, open sores or skin ulcers that itched and hurt, particularly if they occurred in an area subject to abrasion. The condition was common in New Guinea. Most of us suffered from it at one time or another. The usual treatment for the "rot" was to paint the infected area with a solution of potassium permanganate.

My problem at the time of my first exposure was that the medics did not carry permanganate in combat situations. The only suggestion that I received was to keep the infected areas, which were under my arms and between my legs, as clean as possible. Walking caused much discomfort, so when I was not assigned to a patrol, I spent most of the day alternately soaking in the ocean and lying naked, spread-eagled in the sun. After several days the infected areas began to heal, and by the time we were ordered to move out, I was in much better shape. There were times when I had the "rot" again, but that first case was by far the worst.

During the first week at Hollandia I had the opportunity to hear Tokyo Rose, an American-born Japanese propagandist, for the first time. During her broadcasts, which originated in Tokyo, she played sentimental music and hit songs by the big bands of Glenn Miller, Benny Goodman, Tommy Dorsey, and Artie Shaw. She addressed her remarks to us, telling us that our wives and sweethearts were being unfaithful to us while we were fighting in the jungles of New Guinea. The propaganda had an effect opposite to that intended; we enjoyed listening to her. In announcing our attack on Hollandia, she referred to our division as the "Bloody 41st Division Butchers," a nickname that pleased us. In fact, one enterprising GI designed a Christmas card that he somehow had printed before the holiday that year. Many of us purchased the cards, which read "Christmas Greetings from the Southwest Pacific, 1944." They were signed the "41st Division Butchers." A drawing on the cards depicted a large U.S. soldier standing by a chopping block with a carving knife, while a very small Japanese soldier stood shivering before him.

I was told that the name of "Bloody Butchers" was first used by Tokyo Rose after an incident in the Sanananda campaign. The story as related to me involved the capture of a Japanese field hospital by Company G of the 163rd Infantry. As our men approached the hospital, they were fired upon by Japanese soldiers from the hospital tents, inflicting a number of casualties on our troops. Our forces then withdrew, set up machine guns and sprayed the hospital with fire, killing all the occupants.

Originally, the 41st was known as the Sunset Division because of the northwest origins of the division. The division insignia depicted the setting sun over the blue Pacific. It seemed appropriate that the men of the Sunset Division should be fighting against the soldiers of the Rising Sun. The division also was identified by many writers as the Jungleers because of the long, tough battles in the jungles of Papua New Guinea.

It was at Hollandia that Arthur Smith, a member of our platoon, pinned the nickname of Zero on me. Influenced by the Japanese Zero fighter plane, he shortened Catanzaro to Zero, and it became the name by which most of the men knew me. I was amused but not flattered when another GI named Zero appeared in the comic strip "Beetle Bailey" some years later.

It was also during that first week that I went to confession and attended my first "foxhole Mass." I also received the news that I had been promoted to Pfc (private first class). The promotion meant that my pay would increase from $60 to $64.80 per month. About ten days into our stay at Hollandia, another happy event occurred. Mail arrived, and I received fifty letters at one mail call. It was early May, and I was receiving letters written in February and early March. Several days later, I received another forty-four letters. I remember sitting on the beach arranging the letters in chronological order before beginning to read them. I enjoyed every letter that I received, but I was always a little disappointed when a letter was a V-mail form because the letters were so short. V-mail was a one-page 8 x 11–inch form that when folded made its own envelope. The letter was copied and shrunk to half size before being sent to the addressee. V-mail saved shipping space, but it limited the writer to a single page.

Whenever possible, I wrote a letter home at least once a week. My letters were usually short notes because our outgoing mail was censored and we were not allowed to divulge much about our activities or our specific location; but the letters did let my folks know that I was alive and well.

During the time that our perimeter was still set up on the beach, I got my first good look at a live Japanese soldier. One morning while I was sitting near our foxhole, I noticed in the distance what appeared to be five or six men moving along a trail toward our perimeter. Some of the men were carrying long poles topped by dirty white rags. As they neared us, I could see that they were unarmed Japanese soldiers. When they reached our perimeter they were searched and put under guard until they could be taken behind the lines. I remember that they looked very small and young to me. I particularly remember the split-toed, rubber-soled canvas shoes that they wore. The toes of the shoes were divided into two sections, a small one for the big toe and a larger one for the other four. Those shoes did not look very comfortable to me. From the appearance of that scraggly group, I thought the Nips were more to be pitied than feared. Only a few weeks were to pass before my feelings would undergo a radical change.

About a week after D-Day, we received the news that the 186th Infantry had captured the Cyclops and Sentani airdromes on April 26th and linked with the 24th Division, which had captured the Hollandia airdrome the same day. Our forces found a total of 340 Japanese planes[8] that had been destroyed by General George Kenney's Fifth Air Force during raids on the Hollandia airfields between March 30th and April 3rd. The majority of the planes had been destroyed while they were still on the ground. The raids had surprised the Japanese because they thought that Hollandia was not within the range of our fighter planes, which were based in eastern New Guinea. Hollandia was within the range of our heavy bombers, but the Japanese knew that a bombing raid could not be carried out without fighter planes to serve as a cover for the bombers. Unknown to the enemy was the fact that our twin-fuselage P-38 Lightnings had been equipped with auxiliary fuel tanks that brought Hollandia within their range and made the highly successful raids possible.

All the major objectives of the Hollandia campaign were achieved in a much shorter time and with far fewer casualties than had been anticipated. U.S. casualties when the campaign was officially closed were listed as 124 killed, 28 missing, and 1,057 wounded. The Japanese losses were 4,475 killed and 655 captured, an unusually large number of prisoners. The rest of the enemy force,

8. Craven and Cate, eds., *The Pacific,* pp. 592–595.

about 7,000 troops, fled into the jungle. About 6,000 of those are thought to have died trying to reach Wakde, about 125 miles west of Hollandia. During the campaign, our troops freed 125 missionaries, including a number of nuns who had been held since the beginning of the war. Also freed were 120 Sikhs who had been transported from Singapore by the Japanese to serve as slave laborers.

The 163rd Infantry, under the command of General Doe, had also been successful at Aitape, taking their objectives against light enemy resistance. Before being relieved in early May, the 163rd killed 525 Japanese and captured 25. The 163rd Infantry losses were 19 killed and 40 wounded.[9]

It was obvious that the Japanese Army had taken the bait and had moved most of their combat troops from Hollandia to the Wewak–Hansa Bay area to meet the expected assault there. The capture of Hollandia cut off and isolated 180,000 enemy troops. MacArthur and his staff, with the help of intelligence, had outmaneuvered the Japanese generals. We had achieved a spectacular victory at a relatively light cost in lives lost. During the first twenty months of the war in the Southwest Pacific, MacArthur's forces had advanced only about 300 miles, less than one-third of the way, along the New Guinea coast. The landing at Hollandia had advanced the front 500 miles in one bold move.

The operation, however, was not as risky as the code name RECKLESS would imply, because MacArthur's code-breaking organization ULTRA had been successful in breaking the Japanese Army code in the months before the Hollandia landing. Intercepted Japanese radio messages disclosed that three divisions—60,000 men—had been moved from Hollandia to the Hansa Bay area to defend Wewak. The 16,000 Japanese who remained at Hollandia were almost all air force and service troops.[10]

Because it was vital to conceal the fact that the Japanese Army code had been broken, any information learned from intercepted messages was not divulged to anyone other than MacArthur and his immediate staff. Even General Eichelberger, who was in command of all army troops in the Hollandia operation, was not aware of the

9. Smith, *The Approach to the Philippines,* pp. 83, 102, 578.
10. Drea, *MacArthur's ULTRA,* pp. 94, 115–117.

intercepted information. He, like all of us, expected a much stiffer fight.

Our company was very fortunate during the campaign. Most of the fighting took place near the airstrips, about twenty miles from our position. We saw relatively few Japs, and most of those we did see came in waving white flags of surrender. We wondered what our next assignment would be, where it would take us, and how soon it would take place. We did not have to wait long to find out.

The Hollandia campaign had been a huge success, but the airstrips proved to be disappointing. The area around the airdromes was judged to be too swampy for construction of a strip for heavy bombers. A better site west of Hollandia was needed for a major air base that could be used by heavy bombers to support MacArthur's advance toward the Philippines.

Shortly after mid-May, we left our perimeter and moved to White Beach 3 a few miles distant. Once there, we joined other soldiers, who were loading landing craft on the beach. We learned that the 163rd Infantry had already left Aitape and captured Wakde Island, situated offshore the New Guinea coast about 125 miles northwest of Hollandia. Despite the fact that the island was only 3,000 yards long and 1,000 yards wide, it was the site of an airstrip that could be used by heavy bombers. Although the island was taken in two and a half days, it was a tough fight. Seven hundred fifty-nine Japanese were killed; four were taken prisoner. The 163rd Infantry losses were 43 killed and 139 wounded during that short time.[11]

We worked at a feverish pace to complete the loading of the ships. It was clear that we would very soon be aboard a landing craft again. We worked long hours, finally working a twenty-four-hour shift to complete the loading of the last LST.

We had just finished loading the ship and were sitting on the beach when a member of our company who was left behind when we embarked for Hollandia rejoined us. The man had not taken part in the recent landing because shortly before the time to board our LCI, he had broken his glasses. He maintained that he could barely see without his glasses, so he was left behind at Finschhafen. As the GI walked up to report to his squad leader I noticed that he was not wearing glasses; he said that they had been broken aboard the ship that brought him to Hollandia. He reached into his pocket and pulled out the broken glasses to show his squad leader. Without a moment's hesitation the sergeant said, "Don't worry, we'll all be near you when we make the next landing. I'll be sure that you are facing in the right direction." The GI started to protest, but when he saw the look on his squad leader's face, he said no more and dejectedly walked away. His second attempt to avoid combat had failed. Those of us who were watching could not suppress smiles of approval for the sergeant's handling of the situation.

The next morning we received the expected announcement. We would board an LCI the following day to make an assault landing at Biak, one of the Schouten Islands, on May 27th. Biak was described to us as a coral island about forty-five miles long and twenty to twenty-five miles wide. It was located about 350 miles northwest of Hollandia, sixty miles south of the equator in Geelvink Bay, which forms the turkey's neck on the map of New Guinea. The Schouten Islands, we learned, were a part of Dutch New Guinea and were within 900 miles of the Philippine Islands. General Fuller would command the troops that were to be identified as the HURRICANE Task Force. Admiral Fechteler would control the amphibious phases of the landing.

Unlike our briefing for Hollandia, we saw no models or even maps—at least at my level. The description of the assault was simple: the 186th Infantry would establish the beachhead at the village of Bosnek; our 162nd Regiment would follow the 186th ashore and move along a coastal road toward the first of our objectives, the Mokmer airdrome, about nine miles west of the landing site. Two other airstrips, Sorido and Borokoe, were situated just west of the Mokmer airfield. Our 3rd Battalion was named to lead the advance toward the airstrips. Company I would spearhead the 3rd Battalion. We were told that a heavily forested ridge about 300 feet high paralleled the coastal road. The strongest resistance was expected to be at the Mokmer airstrip, our primary objective. The 163rd Infantry would remain at Wakde and would be available as reinforcements, if needed. The stage had been set for the long and bloody battle for the coral hell named Biak.

4

Biak
The HURRICANE Task Force

On the afternoon of May 25th, the members of Company I, fully equipped for combat, trudged up the ramp of an LCI to board the craft that would become part of a convoy that departed that evening for Biak. After the convoy was underway, I went up on deck to eat my evening meal of K-rations. There was a galley aboard the LCI, but it was only large enough to prepare meals for the crew. I was sitting on the deck with several buddies, enjoying the warm breeze, when a member of the ship's crew came out on deck with his mess tray and scraped his leftover food into a barrel. When a second sailor appeared with his tray, one of the men in our company went up to him and asked if he could have the leftovers. The sailor willingly handed him the tray and waited until the GI had eaten the remaining food. Soon a number of other members of our outfit were in line to partake of the leftovers. We had eaten nothing but K-rations for about five weeks; those men would not allow real food, even leftovers, to be dumped into the garbage barrel.

The next morning it was evident that the HURRICANE Task Force on its way to attack Biak was much smaller than the force that had gone ashore at Hollandia. Assault troops were being transported in APDs (destroyer-transports), LSTs, LCTs, and LCIs. Warships escorting the convoy included two heavy cruisers, three light cruisers, and twenty-one destroyers. Because air support was to be provided by Fifth Air Force planes based at Wakde and Hollandia, no aircraft carriers accompanied the task force. The convoy, under the command of Admiral Fechteler, traveled all day and night without incident. The next morning, May 27th, which had been designated Z-day, the convoy stood offshore at Biak.

The bombardment began at 0630, forty-five minutes before the scheduled H-hour 0715. Three cruisers, the *Boise,* the *Nashville,* and the *Phoenix,* shelled the area around the airstrips while the destroyers moved close to the landing beaches to fire on targets at Bosnek. Two waves of B-24 Liberators of the Fifth Air Force took over to complete the barrage of the landing site. B-25 and A-20 attack bombers flew over the area surrounding Bosnek searching for targets. During the shelling, the destroyer *Hutchins* was hit by a 4.7-inch artillery shell that failed to explode, but the shell tore a four-foot hole in the deck, wounding three men.[1]

We watched from our LCI as the 186th Infantry in LVTs and DUKWs (amphibious trucks) moved through the smoke and haze toward the shore. LVTs, called buffaloes, and DUKWs had been chosen to carry the assault waves because those amphibious vehicles were capable of traversing the coral reefs that lay 200 to 600 feet offshore.

After the assault waves had landed, apparently with little or no opposition, our LCI headed toward one of two stone jetties at Bosnek. Because so many gas masks had been thrown overboard before the landing at Hollandia, we were ordered to keep our masks until we reached the beach at Biak. We were instructed that if no gas was evident at that time we should drop the masks on the beach, where they could be recovered easily.

We landed without opposition, dropped our gas masks, and immediately began our advance along the coastal road toward the Mokmer airstrip. As we moved westward, we met members of the 186th Infantry coming toward us. Some of the landing craft used by the assault waves had been carried almost two miles west of the intended landing site by an unexpectedly strong ocean current, and those units were moving eastward to occupy the positions originally assigned to them near the Bosnek beachhead.

---

1. Morison, *New Guinea and the Marianas,* p. 108.

We were able to identify the men as members of the 186th Infantry by the black circles stenciled on the backs of their steel helmets. Members of the 163rd Infantry could be identified by triangles on their helmets; members of the 162nd Regiment, by squares. A letter identifying the company was usually painted next to the symbol. Officers and noncoms wore no identification to show rank, and medics were not identified in any way. Those medics assigned to our company always carried arms. Officers and medics, who were favorite targets of the Japs, looked just like the rest of us.

After a short time, we passed the last members of the 186th Infantry as we advanced steadily along the dirt road toward Mokmer Village. The land to our left could best be described as a swamp. To our right, several hundred yards distant, was a heavily wooded cliff that rose to a height of 300 feet or more. The advance continued with our company at the head of the column. We encountered only light opposition at a water hole, and we all wondered if we would be lucky enough to have another easy victory. As our advance continued, a force of seventy-seven B-24 Liberators bombed the airdrome area.[2]

About mid-afternoon, our squad moved up to spearhead the column. As we advanced, the road moved closer to the ocean, which was to our left, while the cliff to our right angled closer to the coast. Our advance continued until we could see a point about 100 yards ahead where a spur of the cliff extended until it was immediately adjacent to the road. At high tide there was a distance of only about twenty-five feet between the face of the cliff and the ocean, barely enough space for the road. The road then apparently curved to the right beyond the cliff, because we could see nothing but ocean ahead.

After a short discussion, our CO decided to send a patrol out to scout the area, which was later designated as the Parai Defile. With our platoon leader, the gung-ho young second lieutenant, in charge, the first and second squads of our platoon moved out. I was somewhere near the middle of the patrol as the lead scout moved toward the point where the road curved around the cliff. When he reached the defile and cautiously peered around the cliff, gunfire rang out. We had found at least a few Nips who were eager to fight.

2. Morison, *New Guinea and the Marianas*, p. 110.

Our patrol was not in an enviable position. We were protected from any frontal fire by the face of the cliff, which was about twenty feet high, but we were exposed to fire from any Japs who might be on the cliff to our right flank. Only one man could return fire to our front; the rest of us could only hunker down and wait for directions from our platoon leader. After a few minutes he turned to us and said, "Wait here, I'll go get help." While our BAR man Bob Denton laid down covering fire, the lieutenant beat a hasty retreat to the rear.

We waited while Denton periodically fired the BAR around the cliff. When the promised help did not appear, our noncoms decided that we should all try to make our way back to rejoin the company. Running bent over so as to present as small a target as possible, we sped back down the road toward the point where the rest of our company was waiting.

As we made our retreat, Calvin LeMoine was wounded when a Jap bullet creased his skull. When we had rejoined the main body of our outfit we were met with sobering news. Clyde Woods, the leader of the third squad in our platoon, had been killed by the enemy fire. He was the first man in our company to be killed since I joined the outfit. As I looked down at his lifeless body, the reality and finality of the war struck me for the first time. Sergeant Woods, who was a veteran of the long battle at Salamaua, had been killed instantly by a bullet that pierced the front of his steel helmet. The long-barreled Japanese 6.5-mm Arisaka rifles obviously packed a heavy punch. We had been advised to leave our helmet straps unbuckled with the hope that an off-center hit might cause the helmet to spin and deflect a bullet or a piece of shrapnel. However, the bullet that killed Sergeant Woods struck the front of his helmet at almost dead center.

The immediate problem facing us was how to get past the defile and continue our advance toward Mokmer. As we were waiting for a decision on what action should be taken, we were taking occasional fire. A bulldozer and two Sherman tanks that had been following our company moved up to a point near the front of the column. Bulldozers often accompanied tanks in the jungles because it was not unusual to find terrain that tanks could not traverse. The "dozer" was used to clear obstacles so that the tanks could proceed. When faced with the enemy fire that afternoon, the bulldozer operator did not bother to get down from his seat on the bulldozer to join us on the ground; instead, he raised the huge blade of the "dozer" as protection while remaining comfortably seated at the controls. Even though that GI did not seem to worry, the job of the bulldozer operator was not one that I ever envied.

After a short discussion with our CO, the naval fire-support officer accompanying us made radio contact with one of our destroyers to request shelling of the area around the defile. Soon, a destroyer and a rocket LCI bombarded the cliffs at the defile. The tanks also joined in the bombardment, firing from the point at which our advance had been stalled. The hostile fire that we had encountered was silenced, and when the bombardment ended, we prepared to move out again. On the second attempt, with our squad still in the lead, we were able to advance through the defile without further opposition.

Late in the afternoon we reached the village of Parai, a dozen or so native huts built on stilts along the shoreline of a coconut grove. We had advanced about six miles from the beachhead and were within about three miles of the Mokmer airfield. At Parai, a coastal ridge about twenty feet high was positioned north of the grove of coconut trees, most of which had been knocked down or damaged by the barrage preceding the landing. We set up our perimeter for the night on the high ground of the ridge. While we were digging in, eight enemy fighters appeared near Bosnek. Fifth Air Force planes shot down five of the enemy planes but lost one P-47. Just before dusk, four enemy bombers accompanied by several fighter planes bombed and strafed the beachhead area and a number of LSTs unloading cargo at one of the jetties. All of the bombers were shot down by anti-aircraft fire. A single plane, in one of the first kamikaze attacks of the war, dove into the side of a submarine chaser, killing two members of its crew and wounding nine.[3] Shortly after dark, members of our company killed two Japs as they tried to infiltrate our perimeter. The remainder of the night was uneventful in the area immediately surrounding us.

Early the next morning, our platoon leader, the young lieutenant, received a message to report to the company commander. The lieutenant left and after a short time returned, picked up his pack

3. Craven and Cate, *Army Air Forces*, pp. 635–636.

and, without saying a word to anyone, took off down the ridge. We never saw him again. We heard later that the lieutenant had been transferred to the Quartermaster Corps. Apparently, the CO and his executive officer, Lieutenant Goggins, did not look kindly upon the lieutenant's performance under fire the previous afternoon. Our platoon sergeant, Les Perry, was promoted to platoon leader and later received a battlefield commission of second lieutenant.

Shortly after the lieutenant's departure, we received the order to move out. With Company K in the lead, followed by Company I, we began our advance toward the Mokmer airstrip. We moved along the road to Mokmer Village with no opposition. As we left the coconut grove surrounding Mokmer Village, the road climbed a ridge fifteen or twenty feet high, and we found ourselves on a flat coral plateau sparsely covered by small trees and scrub growth. The cliff to our right that had been close to the shoreline had angled away from the coast and was now several hundred yards to the north. To reach the ocean it would be necessary to descend a vertical coral cliff about twenty feet high.

As we moved westward along the road, two of our destroyers sailed abreast of the lead elements of the advancing column. The first indication of trouble was the roar of heavy artillery shells sailing over our heads. I realized that they were enemy shells aimed at our destroyers when spouts of water appeared as the shells landed near the ships. Shortly after that, our forward movement stopped and we heard heavy firing from the direction of the head of the column. The lead elements of Company K had advanced to within 200 yards of the Mokmer airdrome when they were attacked by Japanese infantry and tanks. Our CO ordered the 1st and 3rd Platoons, led by Lieutenants Camack and Madiera, to move up onto the right flank of Company K. The remainder of Company I dispersed just north of the road.

The Japanese artillery continued to fire on our destroyers. One destroyer, the *Stockton,* took a hit on its starboard side, killing one man and wounding another. The other destroyer, the *Reid,* opened fire and temporarily silenced the enemy gun.[4] As we waited, we began to hear heavy fire to our rear. Shortly afterward, we received

4. Morison, *New Guinea and the Marianas,* pp. 114–115.

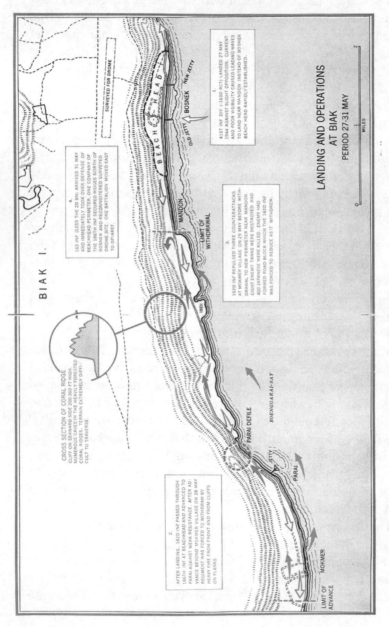

Landing operations at Biak, May 27–31, 1944. From McCartney, *The Jungleers.*

word that the Japs had cut a path between the rear of our battalion and the leading units of the 2nd Battalion at Mokmer Village. All phone lines had been severed. We were cut off and surrounded!

Our situation was perilous at best. The enemy held positions to our front, rear, and right flank. Our left flank was at the top of a steep cliff along the shoreline. Our entire battalion was isolated in an area about 500 yards long and 200 yards deep. Attempts by landing craft to bring supplies or to evacuate wounded were met by artillery fire from the high ridge north of the airstrip. From their positions on the cliffs above, the Japanese could observe our every movement, but our view was limited by the scrub growth. Our company formed a defensive line immediately north of the road in anticipation of an attack from that direction. Mortar fire from the ridge began to fall near our position. It was not possible to dig into the hard coral. We could do nothing but hunker down, watch, and wait.

Suddenly, in rapid order, I heard the sound of two shells exploding immediately to my rear. For the first time I heard the frantic and agonizing cry "Medic!" ring out. I had been prone when the two shells hit the ground. I rose to one knee and looked behind me. There, about eight feet from me, slightly to my right, I saw a black 90-mm mortar shell! The shell, with yellow Japanese characters printed on its outer case, was standing almost upright with its nose buried in the hard coral. I realized that three rounds had been fired; two had exploded, and the third, for some reason known only to the good Lord, had failed to explode. I turned to the man on my right, Bill Key. He had been wounded but was getting to his feet. The man to my left, Arthur Sellers, was also hit by shrapnel. I pointed out the dud and asked him if he could get up. After one look at the shell he said, "Let's get the hell out of here," and rose to his feet. We moved back to a position across the road as medics ministered to several other members of our platoon who had been wounded. Sergeant Stanek, an assistant squad leader in our platoon, was among those wounded by shrapnel.

As the day progressed, our situation worsened. Communications with the destroyers supporting our advance broke down when the naval fire-support officer accompanying us was killed. We were suffering heavy casualties. Landing craft were forced to come to the beach one at a time because they continued to be under artillery fire as they approached the shoreline to bring supplies and evacuate the wounded.

It was an extremely hot day, and by mid-afternoon I had drunk all of my water; I was feeling very tired and thirsty. I saw a cartridge belt with a canteen attached lying on the ground. The belt had been removed from a wounded GI. I picked it up hoping to find water in the canteen, but it was empty. I found a gaping shrapnel hole through the canteen, cup, and cover.

I learned a lot about mortar fire that afternoon. I learned that I could usually hear the hollow "whoomp" of the mortar as the shell left the barrel. I learned also that a mortar shell, unlike an artillery shell, makes no noise as it travels through the air until immediately before reaching its target. Anyone unfortunate enough to be close to the point of impact could usually hear a soft "whoosh" just before the shell landed. When you heard that characteristic sound it was too late to take evasive action.

I also learned that it was wise to begin counting when I heard the first report from a mortar to determine how long it would take for the shell to hit its target. Then, when the second round or set of rounds left the mortar, by counting I could make a reasonable estimate of when the shells would hit the ground. It was imperative to be flat on the ground before the time of impact. Throughout the remainder of the war, the hollow "whoomp" that meant an enemy mortar shell was on its way was a sound I dreaded to hear, but the "whoosh" right before a shell exploded frightened me most. Throughout the rest of the war I often found myself ducking when I heard any sound that closely resembled it.

With the help of four Sherman tanks and the two Company I platoons, Company K had been successful in turning back the attack by the Japanese. As the afternoon wore on, we continued to take heavy mortar fire, but the Japs did not attack again. As dusk approached, we moved to an area north of the road and prepared to set up a perimeter for the night. The outlook was grim. I saw another cartridge belt and canteen on the ground; I picked it up and found that the canteen was in good condition, but it was bone dry. I decided to keep it anyway and hooked it onto my cartridge belt. From that day forward I always carried two canteens. I also decided to keep the ammunition in the cartridge belt. I was certain that we would be under attack that night, and I did not want to run out of ammunition. As we waited for Sergeant Cochran to tell us where to dig in, I was frightened and discouraged, but I was also very angry. We were suffering heavy casualties, but I had not seen a Jap or fired a single shot. I did not look forward to a night attack by the Nips, but at least that seemed better than serving as a target for their mortar shells, which rained out of the sky on us throughout most of that terrifying day.

Spencer Davis, a correspondent for the Associated Press who followed us ashore, was at Mokmer Village that afternoon. His report in *Australia Newsweek* described the situation there.

> By late afternoon Mokmer Village was crowded with maimed and dying American soldiers. Boys with shattered legs, bloody head wounds and faces half shot away were stretched out under every available shelter. . . . With shocking frequency, I saw medical aides shake their heads and draw a blanket over a shattered form. Most of the seriously wounded were victims of the wicked Japanese knee mortars. Some men without a scratch—dazed and shocked and speechless—huddled in the shade.

The report by Spencer Davis was accurate, I believe, with one exception. Most of the casualties were not victims of knee mortars, which fired a 50-mm grenade, but rather of the much larger 90-mm mortars fired from caves in the cliffs that towered above us.

Before trying to dig in for the night, I made another attempt to get some water. There was a very small puddle at the side of the road. It was shallow, but I was able to get some muddy liquid into my canteen cup. I took a dirty handkerchief out of my pocket and tried to filter some of the mud out of the slurry. I had little success, but because I was so thirsty, I tried to down some of the liquid anyway. It tasted awful; I could not drink it. In a final attempt to down the sludge, I took a packet of lemonade mix from my K-rations and tried to dissolve it in the liquid in my cup. It was to no avail. I still could not swallow it.

Just before dusk, we received an order to prepare to move out. We were going to try to break through the roadblock to our rear. When word was given, we started to retrace our steps along the road toward Mokmer Village, nearly a mile from our present position.

As we approached the spot where the enemy had penetrated our lines, I saw two Sherman tanks positioned north of the road laying down covering fire for us. I was more than happy to see them. Surely their presence greatly improved our chances of breaking through the roadblock.

When we received the word, we took off at full speed to run the gauntlet of Japanese mortar, machine-gun, and rifle fire in an attempt to rejoin the rest of the regiment at Mokmer Village. I was not one of the largest or strongest men in our outfit, but I could run. I feel certain that on that evening no one ran faster than I did. Nothing slowed me down. I ran at full speed through the brush along the road, leaping over the trunks of fallen trees like a high hurdler in a track meet. As I raced down the last ridge into the perimeter of the 2nd Battalion at Mokmer Village, a feeling of great relief and safety came over me. I don't think I could have felt better or more safe if I had been at home. The saying "everything is relative" took on new meaning for me.

After the last living member of our battalion had reached the coconut grove, four Sherman tanks came down the ridge and parked close to the spot where I was sitting. Each tank had a name stenciled on its side. I can recall two of the names, "Sad Sack" and "Murder Inc." A member of the crew of "Murder Inc." climbed out of his tank, turned to me, and said, "Kind of tough up there today, wasn't it?" I nodded in agreement and said, "Yeah." As we continued our conversation, he told me that a number of Japanese tanks had taken part in the attack on Company K earlier in the day and that three of our tanks had been damaged by enemy artillery fire. The young crew member said that our tanks had fired on the enemy tanks at long range but had done little damage. He said he hoped that the Japanese tanks would attack again tomorrow. "If they do," he said, "they won't escape a second time."

After we had received our rations and the desperately needed water we were ready to bed down. But before we could begin to dig in, we were told that additional men were needed to fill out the perimeter on the ridge above Mokmer Village. Our platoon was chosen to provide the men to fill the gap in that perimeter. The rest of the company would stay in the coconut grove. My morale sank as we climbed the ridge in near darkness. It had been a disastrous day for us. We had been able to evacuate all the wounded, but for the only time throughout the war, we were forced to leave some of our dead behind. I particularly remember the body of Humbird Dunlap, a member of our company, lying in a ditch at the side of the road as we made our retreat. His face was covered with dust from the road, his glasses were askew, and one of his arms had been crushed by the caterpillar treads of one of our tanks. The bodies of our fallen comrades were not recovered until about two weeks later.

As I prepared to bed down, I noticed a hole in my loose-fitting fatigue jacket. Apparently a piece of shrapnel or a bullet had come very close earlier that day. We were not able to dig into that hard coral on the ridge, so we piled chunks of coral around us for protection. As I prepared to stand the first watch, I thanked the good Lord for watching over me that day and asked for His protection through the night.

The night passed without incident in our immediate area of the perimeter, but early the next morning the Japs renewed their attack from the west down the coastal road. Our platoon was still on the ridge north of the road and about 100 yards east of the point of the assault. We could not see the battle that took place, but we could hear the machine-gun, rifle, and mortar fire as the 2nd Battalion turned back the Japanese infantrymen. A second Japanese attack shortly afterward was led by four tanks, followed closely by infantry. As the enemy tanks came down the hill from the terrace into the coconut grove, they were greeted by fire from two Sherman tanks of the 603rd Tank Company. The light Japanese tanks armed with 37-mm guns were no match for the heavily armored Sherman tanks and their 75-mm cannons; in the first tank battle of the war in the Pacific, all four enemy tanks were destroyed and the attack was thwarted.

After a short pause, the Japanese attacked again, this time led by three tanks. By then a third Sherman tank had joined the battle. As in the previous battle, the Japanese tanks were quickly destroyed and the infantry assault was turned back. One U.S. tank was slightly damaged by an enemy shell, but several other hits on our tanks caused little damage.[5]

The situation worsened shortly after that when a short round fired by one of our destroyers landed in the coconut grove immedi-

5. Smith, *MacArthur's Approach*, p. 310.

ately below our position on the cliff, killing five men and wounding thirty-one others. Among those casualties were twelve members of Company I, including Mess Sergeant John Alberghina and Richard Thorne, who were killed, and Lieutenant Ward Madeira, who lost his right arm. His arm was so badly damaged that a medic used a knife to amputate the arm while the lieutenant lay on the beach.[6]

The Japanese infantry abandoned their frontal attacks and began to circle north of our position on the ridge in an attempt to close the coastal road behind us. They were successful in setting up a roadblock at a point east of Parai, but a counterattack by Company B and Cannon Company of the 162nd Infantry drove them off and reopened the road.

Shortly after noon, we learned that Colonel Harold Haney, commander of the 162nd Infantry, had ordered the withdrawal of the entire regiment. We would fall back along the road to the east until we could make contact with the 186th Regiment near the original beachhead. The retreat began with Company I leading the 3rd Battalion, but our platoon stayed on the ridge with Company L as the rear guard for the regiment. As we waited, hoping that the Nips would not attack again, it seemed that the column of retreating GIs was endless. Finally, when the last of our troops had moved back down the road, we received the word to move out.

We scrambled down the ridge, raced through the coconut grove past the disabled enemy tanks with their dead crews, and hurriedly followed the rest of our troops down the road toward Bosnek. We had gone only a short distance when we came to a section of 4.2-inch mortars that had been supplying welcome and much-needed covering fire for our withdrawal. One of the men asked, "How far back are the front lines?" When he was told, "You're looking at the front lines," he and his men, members of Company D 641st Tank Destroyer Battalion, went into frenzied action. Each of their six mortars weighed 315 pounds, so they could not be hand-carried easily. The mortars had to be destroyed. After smashing the sights and dropping thermite grenades down the barrels, the men fell in line behind us as we hurried along the road.[7]

6. Westerfield, *41st Infantry Division*, pp. 129, 149.
7. Smith, *MacArthur's Approach*, p. 307.

Our hasty retreat continued until we reached Parai, where we came upon the unexpected but welcome sight of LVTs waiting at the shore. We climbed aboard, and the buffaloes moved offshore until out of range of enemy guns. Then the slow-moving craft headed toward Bosnek, the site of our initial landing two days earlier. It was raining as the amphibious vehicles began the six-mile trip eastward along the coast.

During the trip everyone was silent, and I relived the events of the last two and a half days in my mind. I could picture that black 90-mm mortar shell with its bright yellow printing, and I could not help wondering if I would be alive if it had exploded. I also thought about what I had felt was my bad luck when I was ordered onto that ridge the night before the destroyer shelled the coconut grove. Was it an order that saved my life? I knew that my family and friends at home were saying a lot of prayers for my safety. As we neared Bosnek, I remembered that the previous day, May 28th, was my sister Margaret's eighteenth birthday. It was a day I will never forget.

MacArthur and his chief of staff, General Richard Sutherland, received deserved praise for planning the Hollandia campaign; however, it was obvious to those of us involved that the kindest thing that could be said about the plan for the capture of Biak was that it was overly optimistic. Our regiment had suffered 220 casualties, including 33 killed on the first three days, and our battalion had narrowly escaped annihilation. Although about 400 enemy soldiers had been killed during that period, even a green Pfc such as I could see that we could not take the airstrips until the Nips were cleared from the ridges north of them.[8]

The next morning, because of the heavy losses we had suffered on the first three days, it was necessary to make changes in the organization of our platoon. Instead of the normal three squads, our platoon had barely enough men to make up two squads. I was assigned to a squad led by Sergeant George Cooley. My new squad leader, a soft-spoken, likeable man from Bend, immediately informed me that I would be the second scout for the squad. This news surprised me because I remembered being told during basic training that only the most experienced and most able men would be chosen to be

8. Smith, *MacArthur's Approach*, pp. 307, 311.

scouts. I did not think that I met either qualification; nevertheless, I served as second scout during the remainder of the battle for Biak.

Our 3rd Battalion was now in position near Ibdi about two miles west of Bosnek, and we began patrolling the high ground north of the coastal road. We found coral ridges heavily forested by large trees, long trailing vines, heavy undergrowth, and, in most areas, limited visibility. At times, the lead scouts had to use machetes to clear a path through the undergrowth. As we moved through the jungle on one of those patrols, a snake, probably about four feet long, fell out of a tree onto the pack of a GI a short distance in front of me. The man immediately behind him knocked the snake off with his rifle and we moved on.

As we advanced in single file up the steep native track called Young Man's Trail, I heard several shots ring out directly behind me. I turned to find that Stacy Wilson, the man following me, had just killed a Jap within a few feet of the trail. I, and the twenty or more men who had preceded me, had passed within an arm's distance of the Nip without seeing him. He had been hiding in a spider hole dug beneath the roots of a large tree. As we had advanced that afternoon, Stacy had for some reason lagged, leaving a larger-than-normal gap in the column. As he came around a curve in the trail, he saw the Jap starting to get out of his hole and shot him. It was not uncommon for the Japanese to let an entire unit pass and then attack the rear of the column. Whether that particular servant of the emperor thought I was the last man in the column and intended to shoot me or just wanted to make a getaway, I will never know; but I believe that if his intention had been to escape, he would have waited at least a little longer.

The next morning I awoke with chills and fever; I felt terrible. I sought out the medic assigned to our platoon; he took my temperature and said I had a fever of 103.6°F. He told me to gather my gear and report to the first aid station at Bosnek. As I started to hike the two miles back to the aid station, I felt miserable but happy. I expected that I would be sent to a hospital somewhere behind the lines. It was an opportune time, I thought, to get sick.

When I reached the battalion aid station, I sat on the ground outside a tent and waited for the doctor, who eventually appeared. He looked at me, asked me how I felt, and took my temperature. He confirmed the fact that I had a very high fever and said that I probably had malaria. He told me that the field hospital was overloaded with casualties; there was no room for someone with nothing worse than malaria. He handed me a bottle of Atabrine, a synthetic quinine, and told me to take six pills a day instead of the usual dose of two pills until I felt better. Still feeling terrible, but now quite discouraged, I started back down the road to rejoin my outfit.

When I reached the perimeter, I learned that two battalions of the 163rd Infantry had moved from Wakde to Biak and had taken over the defense of the beachhead, freeing the 186th Infantry to take part in the drive on the Mokmer airstrip. The plan, as explained to us, was for the 186th plus the 2nd Battalion of the 162nd Infantry to advance westward along a plateau north of the coastal ridges, while our 3rd Battalion would try again to move along the coastal road toward Mokmer. The cliffs that formed the Parai Defile had been bombed and strafed by air force planes and had been shelled by warships. It was expected that we would find resistance weakened or eliminated when we reached that point again.

The next morning, June 1st, the new plan was put into action. That date marked the beginning of the only period during the war that the entire division fought as a unit. The 186th Infantry began its advance on the plateau while our battalion moved along the road toward the defile. As the lead elements of our battalion approached the defile they met heavy enemy fire and were forced to withdraw. The bombardment of the Parai Defile was resumed with renewed fury.

The following day, without opposition, Company A of the 163rd Infantry seized two small islands, Owi and Mios Wendi.[9] Owi lay about three miles offshore of Bosnek, and Mios Wendi was situated about ten miles to the southeast. Immediately after the seizure of Owi, engineers started construction of an airstrip and a field hospital on the island. Mios Wendi was quickly put into use as a base for PT boats (patrol vessels, motor torpedo boats) operating in the area.

On several occasions after our return to the area near Ibdi, Japanese planes made low-level raids during daylight hours. One day we were strafed by one of our own B-25s. On most nights

9. Smith, *MacArthur's Approach,* p. 341.

"Washing-Machine Charlie," our nickname for Japanese bombers, paid us a visit. The nickname was chosen because the pulsating sound of the bombers' motors resembled the sound of a washing machine. One night a Nip bomber dropped a parachute flare, which lit up the area immediately around us with a bright greenish-white light for an unbelievably long time. Anti-aircraft guns were fired at the flare in an unsuccessful attempt to knock it down. I waited for bombs to fall or a banzai attack to materialize; thankfully, neither occurred. However, later that night, Sergeant Norman Smith was killed by a grenade as a small group of Nips tried unsuccessfully to infiltrate our perimeter.

Apparently, the Japanese had decided to make an all-out fight for Biak because on June 2nd, fifty-four enemy planes attacked the beachhead and our ships offshore. The following day, forty-one enemy planes attacked. The Japs lost twenty-three aircraft during those raids while inflicting only minor damage on our ships.[10]

The next day, June 4th, we received more devastating news. A large Japanese naval force, including a battleship, four cruisers, and eight destroyers transporting 2,500 troops, had been sighted by one of our planes. The warships were headed toward Biak with the intent to bombard our beachhead and land reinforcements. Furthermore, we were told that the only U.S. naval force capable of engaging the enemy fleet could not reach Biak until several hours later than the enemy convoy was expected to arrive. To prepare for the attack, bulldozers dug gun pits so artillery could be repositioned to fire seaward. The situation could hardly have looked worse. I was still sick, we were making no progress against the enemy already on the island, and now we faced the prospect of a naval bombardment and the landing of enemy reinforcements.

The convoy was expected to arrive by late afternoon, but the afternoon passed and no enemy ships appeared. Just before nightfall, we were told that the enemy fleet had turned back. Apparently, a Japanese reconnaissance plane had mistakenly reported that a large U.S. naval force, including battleships and aircraft carriers, was at Biak. However, there were no warships larger than destroyers in the area at that time. We had been saved by an incorrect

10. Morison, *New Guinea and the Marianas*, pp. 119–122.

identification by a Japanese pilot, who probably mistook LSTs for
aircraft carriers and destroyers for battleships. A large force of our
bombers was sent to attack the enemy convoy, but our planes were
unable to locate the enemy warships. Our naval force also failed to
make contact, but we were all greatly relieved as we tried to dig
into the hard coral that evening.[11]

Over the next several days, our battalion made repeated attempts
to penetrate the Parai Defile. By that time, however, the Japanese
had strengthened their defenses; despite continued bombardments
by air force planes, artillery, and naval units, strong enemy resistance continued. There was some good news, however; we learned
that Rome had fallen to U.S. troops. Also, the increased dosage of
Atabrine had been effective; my temperature had returned to normal
and I was feeling a lot better.

A decision by General Fuller to bypass the Parai Defile was put
into action on the afternoon of June 7th. After an artillery and
naval bombardment, with Companies I and K making up the assault waves in LVTs, a landing was made west of the defile near
Parai Village. As soon as we landed, we began to come under mortar fire from the high ridge to the north. We were followed ashore
by six tanks and supporting troops of Cannon Company. By this
time it was late afternoon, and we prepared to dig in for the night.

Before we set up our perimeter, we discovered a number of un-
opened cartons of ten-in-one rations that had been left behind by
some of our service troops when the entire regiment had made the
withdrawal on the afternoon of May 29th. Each carton contained a
day's ration for ten men. We had eaten nothing but K-rations for
about six weeks, so we eagerly opened the large cartons and divided those much tastier rations among ourselves. From the varied
items in one of the boxes, I chose a can containing real bacon. The
next morning I burned the straps off my steel helmet while using
it as a frying pan to cook the bacon. It was worth it, though; my
buddies and I really enjoyed the bacon.

Later that morning, the 1st Battalion and the remainder of our
3rd Battalion landed at Parai and we began an advance toward the
Mokmer airdrome to reinforce the 186th Infantry, which had occu-

pied the airstrip on June 7th. The 186th Infantry, reinforced by the 2nd Battalion 162nd Infantry, had reached the airdrome by way of the plateau behind the ridges to the north and had established a perimeter near the coast. However, they were suffering heavy casualties caused by artillery and mortar fire from enemy positions on the high ground north of Mokmer airdrome.

Our advance that morning began with Companies I and K climbing the low coastal cliff north of the road. Then we started to move westward along a plateau while Company C advanced along the coastal road. We encountered no opposition until early afternoon, when we came under heavy mortar fire from the area on the high ridge to the north, later identified as the East Caves.

During the mortar attack, while I was trying to dig into the hard coral with little success, several mortar shells hit to my left and the cry of "Medic!" rang out. No medics appeared, and the calls for help continued. The wounded man was about thirty or forty yards away. I decided that I should try to help. I got up and had just started to run toward the man when I saw two medics nearing him, so I turned and headed back to the place where I had left my pack. I had just returned to my position when more shells hit to my right. I knew that normal procedure when directing fire was to bracket the target, then to "fire for effect" into the center of the bracketed area. Of course, trying to predict where the next rounds would fall was a deadly game of chance, but in that instance I decided to move to a new position while our artillery tried to silence the enemy mortars. I moved several times that afternoon trying to outguess the Japanese mortarmen until, thankfully, we received the order to withdraw.

As we began to retrace our steps, Ernie Gallo called out to me, "Zero, look at my back. It feels like something is sticking in it." I raised his pack and saw a bloody fatigue shirt with a ragged hole in it. Ernie, one of the smallest and oldest men in the company, had been wounded by shrapnel and did not know it; his pack had probably saved his life. Ernie was one of nine Company I casualties that afternoon. Two of the men, Frank Titting and Lincoln "Power House" Williams, were killed. June 8th had been another demoralizing day.

That evening we received the news about D-Day on the beaches of Normandy. The news was welcome, of course, but we were much too concerned with our immediate situation to dwell on the progress of the war in Europe.

Unknown to us at that time, the Japanese Navy undertook a second attempt to reinforce their troops on Biak. On June 7th, a naval force of six destroyers with troops aboard departed Sorong, heading for Biak. Some of the destroyers towed barges that carried additional troops. The Japanese force was sighted by P-38s and B-25s flying out of Hollandia. Our planes sank one destroyer, the *Harusame,* and damaged three others, but the five remaining ships continued on course toward Biak. The U.S. Navy was alerted, and a force of eight destroyers and two cruisers set out from Hollandia to intercept the Japanese convoy. Shortly before 2400 on June 8th, the U.S. naval force sighted the enemy ships approaching the north coast of Biak. The Japanese ships that were towing barges cut them loose and fled, with the U.S. destroyers giving chase. Two of the Japanese destroyers were damaged before the chase was broken off. One of the barges was sunk; some of the other barges may have reached Biak.[12] The second Japanese attempt to reinforce Biak was essentially a failure.

The next day, June 9th, we tried again to advance toward the airstrip. Despite the fact that we were reinforced by two tanks, we were pinned down by mortar fire again and were forced to fall back.

I always looked upon the presence of the tanks as a mixed blessing. It was comforting to have the additional firepower, but the noise created by the tanks certainly removed any chance of surprising the Japs. Also, the tanks usually drew fire by any Nips within range. I particularly disliked the situation when Stacy and I were leading the column as scouts. It was standard operating procedure for a squad of men to precede the tanks because the Japs had been known to attack tanks and kill crew members by climbing on the tanks and dropping grenades into open ports or attaching magnetic mines to the hulls of the tanks. Nevertheless, I always thought that the tanks and their crews were in less danger than we were. I would have been much happier if the tanks had been up front leading the column while we protected them from the rear.

Because we continued to draw such heavy fire from the East

Caves, Colonel Haney decided to abandon our attempts to advance along the road or the terrace north of the road. Instead, on June 10th, our battalion began to move along the shore behind the coastal cliffs that afforded protection from enemy fire along much of the way. As we moved out, I noticed a plane flying just above the ocean coming toward us. When it neared, I saw something fall from the plane. I assumed that it was a bomb, but it was only an empty auxiliary fuel tank, dropped by one of our A-20 attack bombers. I breathed a sigh of relief and moved on.

To reach the airstrip, which was three miles distant, it was necessary to wade through the ocean much of the way. This created a painful problem for me because I no longer had socks to wear. I had started with two pair when we made the Hollandia landing. Both pair had worn through and been discarded. At that time we did not as yet have combat boots. We wore leggings, but the sharp coral at Biak cut through the straps that fit under the insteps of my boots, making the leggings useless. I had thrown them away, too. As we waded along the shoreline, sand began to collect in my boots. Each time the column stopped I removed my boots and washed the sand out, but by the time we reached the Mokmer airstrip late that afternoon, my feet had been rubbed raw.

As soon as we reached the eastern end of the airstrip, we started to advance swiftly toward the ridge to the north. We reached the high ground near the eastern end of the low ridge overlooking the airstrip without drawing enemy fire and began to set up our perimeter for the night. The vegetation in the surrounding area was rather sparse, and we had an unusually clear view of the area surrounding our perimeter.

We had just finished digging our shallow hole and I was sitting on the ground when I noticed movement about 100 yards north of our perimeter. As I watched, I saw a Japanese soldier stand up and then, using his rifle as a cane, hobble toward a more heavily wooded area to the north. I reached for my rifle and knelt to take aim. As I brought my M1 up to my shoulder, I heard several shots ring out, and the Jap fell to the ground. One more servant of the emperor had made the supreme sacrifice.

I wondered why the man had not waited another hour until darkness had fallen, when he could have easily escaped. Either he was not aware of our presence or he was committing hara-kiri in a nontraditional way. As I sat in my hole, I was thankful that someone had squeezed his trigger before I had been able to fire my rifle. No Jap could be allowed to escape, but to this day I am glad that I had not been the one to kill that particular Jap who was trying to escape using a "cane."

A week earlier, when the 186th Infantry had reached the position we now occupied, Colonel Oliver Newman, commander of the 186th Infantry, requested permission to clear the ridge overlooking the Mokmer airdrome before occupying the airstrip, but he was ordered by General Fuller to take the airfield and secure it. General Fuller undoubtedly ordered that course of action because he was being pressured by General Walter Krueger, commander of the Sixth Army, to do so. It was a poor decision, because as soon as the 186th Infantry set up a perimeter on the beach, they began to suffer heavy casualties caused by enemy fire from the ridge. Now our 3rd Battalion had the assignment to clear the Nips from that ridge.

The next day, June 11th, our company led the advance to the west in an effort to displace the 600 to 700 Japs who occupied the ridge. We met stubborn resistance immediately. Numerous enemy pillboxes constructed of logs and coral were positioned along the ridge. Tanks could not be used in the rugged terrain, and we found it difficult to dislodge the Japs. We were held up for the greater part of that day by machine-gun fire from a pillbox.

The following morning, a flame thrower was brought up from the rear and we prepared to attack the pillbox again. The operator with his flame thrower, which weighed about sixty-five pounds, accompanied our squad as we crawled along the south side of the ridge to flank the enemy position and get close enough so that the pillbox would be within range of the flame thrower. We moved slowly and carefully along the steep side of the ridge until we reached a point that satisfied the GI with the flame thrower. I was immediately to his right, and he turned to me and said, "Get ready. When I spray the pillbox they'll come running out." He stood up and sprayed the pillbox with napalm. We waited, but no Nips appeared. They had abandoned the pillbox during the night.

We continued to advance slowly to the west against strong emplacements and stubborn resistance. During the afternoon we suffered a number of casualties while attacking another pillbox. Julius Murkli, one of the wounded, later died as a result of his wounds.[13]

That evening, as we prepared to set up our perimeter for the night, Stacy Wilson and I decided to set up a booby trap in the jungle in front of our foxhole. Booby traps were usually set up by tying a hand grenade to a tree trunk at a point very close to the ground. One end of a cord was then tied to the ring of the grenade, and the other end was tied to a second tree so that anyone walking or crawling toward our hole would hit the cord and pull the pin from the grenade.

It was beginning to get dark as we started to set up the trap. We told the men in the holes adjacent to ours what we were going to do so that they would not mistakenly fire on us. I took the grenade and tied it to a tree and tied my end of the cord to the ring of the grenade. I also straightened the cotter pin of the grenade so it would pull out easily if the cord were to be tripped. I held the handle of the grenade down with one hand, and I had a finger of my other hand through the ring while Stacy attached his end of the cord to a tree. When he had completed fastening the cord, Stacy gave me a sign and I took my finger out of the ring. To my dismay the ring and the attached pin flew out of the grenade and into the jungle.

By this time it was getting darker. I couldn't retrieve the pin because I had to hold down the handle of the grenade so that it would not explode. When Stacy realized what had happened, he went back and followed the cord from his end until he found the ring and pin. After some difficulty I was able to insert the pin in the handle and tighten it enough so that when I took my finger from the ring the pin stayed in the handle. The next morning the grenade was still in place. I cut it loose from the tree, bent the pin farther back to tighten it, and hung the grenade on my pack alongside the other grenades I was carrying. That was the first and last time I was involved in setting up a booby trap.

A short time later that morning, I was picked to be part of a six-man reconnaissance patrol. We were never asked to volunteer for patrols or other duties during combat. A squad leader was usually assigned to lead small patrols, and he chose the men he wanted to accompany him. Those assigned to the patrol accepted the assign-

13. Westerfield, *41st Infantry Division*, p.150.

ment willingly, if not enthusiastically. Our objective that morning was to move westward along the ridge to scout the area ahead in an attempt to determine the location of any pillboxes. We moved out and had progressed about 100 yards when we saw a high point on the ridge about thirty yards ahead. George Cooley, who was leading the patrol, ordered us to hold up. He and Arthur Smith went ahead to what appeared to be a good observation point. The rest of the patrol waited in place. I was the next forward man. As I stood waiting I was looking to my right, where the ground fell off slightly from the top of the ridge.

As I watched, the head and upper body of a Japanese soldier appeared. He was probably twenty-five or thirty yards to my right and was moving very slowly and cautiously in the opposite direction to which our patrol was headed. He was almost directly abreast of me, which meant that he had already passed George and Smitty. He looked exactly like Japs I had seen in movies. He wore glasses, and his helmet was covered with netting that held sprigs of green foliage. He carried a long Arisaka rifle with a shiny fixed bayonet.

I aimed my rifle at him; he was so close and moving so slowly I knew I could not miss, but several thoughts flashed through my mind. Was he the first scout or had others preceded him? Was he a member of a small patrol or a larger attacking force? If I fired, would the two men ahead be cut off or would all six of us be in dire straits? If we were to come under attack by a large enemy force, our only course of action would be to retrace our steps along the ridge. The seaward face of the cliff at that point was so steep that going down the cliff was not an option. As I stood there with my rifle aimed at the Nip, the decision was taken out of my hands. George and Smitty, who had also spotted the Japs, sped by me heading back to our perimeter. As they passed me George said, "Come on!" Suddenly the Jap dropped out of my sight. I'm certain he heard the noise as the two men hurried past me. I wasted no time following my buddies back toward our perimeter.

When we reached it, we spread the word that the Japs were headed toward us. We hunkered down and waited. From my position in the perimeter, I could not see the Japs when they appeared to my right a few minutes later. They were greeted with heavy fire, and four members of the enemy force were slain. It was a pleasant change that day to be able to lie in wait for the Nips rather than to be always on the attack while they waited for us.

We dug in that night with a dead Japanese soldier within the perimeter. He had been dead for several days, and no one wanted to move him. Because it was almost impossible to dig a hole on the ridge, his fellow soldiers had sprinkled lime over his body. I can still picture him lying on his back with his right hand up to his throat. I was not happy to have him so close to our foxhole.

In spite of two failures in attempts to reinforce Biak, the commander of the Japanese Mobile Fleet, Admiral Jisaburo Ozawa, was still determined to land reinforcements and hold Biak. On June 11th, he assembled a force so powerful that success would be assured. The force gathered at Batjan included two super battleships—the world's largest, two heavy cruisers, a light cruiser, three destroyers, and six transports. The two battleships, the *Yamato* and the *Musashi*, 863 feet each in length, were clad with sixteen inches of armor and carried 18.1-inch guns capable of firing 3,220-pound shells a distance of thirty miles.

The plan was to land the reinforcements at Biak on June 15th and deliver a crippling bombardment against U.S. troops on both Biak and Owi. However, the next day, June 12th, U.S. air attacks against Guam and Saipan caused a change in the Japanese plans; Admiral Ozawa was ordered to move the fleet north in anticipation of a U.S. landing on Saipan.[14] It was the end of Japanese attempts to reinforce Biak. Because of the Saipan invasion, we had narrowly escaped what could have been a disastrous encounter with the Japanese fleet.

Although it was now mid-June, the Mokmer airstrip was still not in use except by the single-engine Piper Cub planes used by the artillery spotters. Every attempt by the members of our engineering corps to repair the runways was met by enemy artillery fire from high ground north of the ridge we were trying to clear. We watched as the shells exploded on the strip below after sailing over our heads. Our view from the ridge was the same one that the enemy had used to their advantage on that disastrous second day of the campaign. Almost three weeks had passed since the landing.

The original plan called for capture of the Mokmer strip in three days. General Fuller requested another regiment as reinforcements, and the 34th Infantry of the 24th Division was alerted for movement to Biak.

General MacArthur was impatient with the slow progress and pressured General Walter Krueger, who, in response to the pressure, ordered General Eichelberger to Biak to replace General Fuller as commander of the forces on Biak. When General Eichelberger arrived at Biak on June 15th, General Fuller, feeling that he had been unfairly treated by General Krueger, requested that he be relieved of command of the 41st Division. General Eichelberger tried to persuade General Fuller, a longtime friend, to stay on as commander of the division but was unable to do so. General Fuller was relieved of his command, and General Doe, the commander of our 163rd Regiment, was then promoted to division commander.

As a farewell, General Fuller addressed the following letter to members of his division:

16 June 1944

To the Officers and Men of the Forty-first Infantry Division.

1. I am being relieved of command for my failure to achieve the results demanded by higher authority. This is in no way a reflection upon you or your work in this operation. I, and I alone, am to blame for this failure.

2. I have commanded the Forty-first Division for better or worse for over two years and a half. During that period I have learned to respect you, to admire you, and to love you, individually and collectively. You are the finest body of men that it has been my privilege to be associated with in thirty-nine years of service.

3. I part with you with many pangs of heart. I wish all of you the best of luck and God Bless You, for I love you all.[15]

General Fuller was reassigned and became deputy chief of staff at the headquarters of Admiral Lord Louis Mountbatten's Southeast Asia Command, where he served capably during the rest of the war.

Shortly afterward, we were told that General Eichelberger

15. Smith, *MacArthur's Approach,* pp. 343–344. Quote on p. 344.

would be coming to the front to make a personal assessment of the situation. Our CO decided that a six-man escort should be chosen to serve as a guard for the general. At that stage of the campaign, most of us were rather sorry sights. I had no leggings or socks, I had discarded my underwear, I had a hole in my fatigue jacket, and I had burned the straps off my steel helmet; nevertheless, I was chosen to be a member of the guard unit. That I was chosen as one of the most presentable members of the company should tell a lot about the condition of our entire outfit. Our company, originally about 180 men strong, was probably down to a strength of 80 or 85 men at that time.

The next day, members of the guard unit, all cleanly shaven, waited in place on the ridge for General Eichelberger; but to our disappointment, he never arrived at our perimeter. However, in his book *Our Jungle Road to Tokyo,* the general describes his visit to the front lines that afternoon. Apparently he had been very close, but he was unable to reach our perimeter because a firefight was in progress near our position.

I remember only one officer of higher rank than our company commander who often appeared at the front. That man was our battalion commander, Major Paul Hollister. He was a middle-aged man who carried 250 pounds on his rather short, stocky frame. His appearance and actions belied the fact that he was the commanding officer of an infantry battalion; he looked as dirty and disheveled as the rest of us. He was an officer who led by his presence and example. Men followed him without question; everyone admired his willingness to share the danger of the front lines with us.

One evening during our fight to clear that ridge overlooking the airstrip, a surprising and happy event occurred. We had just finished digging in for the night when, unbelievably, freshly baked bread and steaming hot coffee suddenly arrived at our perimeter. I don't know where the bread and coffee were made—probably on a ship offshore—but I do know that it was one of the most enjoyable meals I have ever eaten. I have never forgotten that wonderful unexpected treat.

Another unusual incident took place on that ridge early one morning. It was shortly after daybreak when all of us were still in our foxholes. I was awake, completing the last guard watch of the night. One of the men in the next hole called out to let me know that he was going to get out of his hole to relieve himself. He moved eight or ten feet outside the perimeter, dropped his pants and began to squat. I was not paying any attention until I heard some thrashing in the undergrowth. I turned in time to see the GI wildly crawling, his trousers around his ankles, back toward his foxhole. He reached the hole and dived in. The undergrowth was very thick around us and I could see nothing unusual. In answer to my question he said that he had just dropped his pants when he heard a noise and, looking up, found himself face to face with a Jap soldier. Apparently the Nip was alone and was as startled as the GI. The Jap quickly disappeared into the jungle while the GI scrambled back toward his foxhole. Surely that was the ultimate example of being caught with one's pants down.

That evening we found a dead Jap within a few yards of the spot where we were told to dig our hole for the night. Because the Nip was so close to our perimeter we decided to try to cover the body with dirt and coral. The man was lying on his side and one arm was slightly raised. We scraped enough dirt off the coral to cover all of the man's body but his arm. While one man pushed the arm down, the rest of us gathered enough large chunks of coral to hold the arm down. A few more shovels of dirt were added, and the job was completed. However, the next morning as I sat in our hole while the sun was rising, I could see an arm pointing toward the heavens from that shallow grave. I knew about the effects of rigor mortis, but the sight of that arm pointing upward gave me an eerie feeling. I was happy when we moved on that morning.

Before we had embarked for the Hollandia invasion, I had filled a small waterproof plastic container with about two dozen matches. I had put the container in my pack and decided that I would not use any of the matches until someone in our platoon needed a match and no one else had any. I carried the matches through all of the Hollandia campaign and most of the battle for Biak. Late one rainy afternoon after we had dug in for the night on the ridge, Smitty wanted to heat a cup of water for coffee, but he could find no one with any dry matches. My time to be a hero had arrived. I reached into my pack and presented the waterproof container to Smitty. My moment of glory was short-lived, however. With growing disappointment, Smitty tried without success to light every match in the case. The humidity had ruined my matches. In a minute or two I had been transformed from hero to goat. I took a lot of verbal abuse from Smitty that evening as he washed down his corned pork and hardtack biscuits with luke-warm water rather than hot coffee.

Water was so hard to find on Biak that on most days it had to be brought up to us from points behind the front lines. The water was usually transported in five-gallon metal cans. One day when we were still fighting on the ridge, our water supply did not arrive. Because we desperately needed the water, arrangements were made late that afternoon to send a patrol to pick it up. I was one of twenty men chosen to be a member of that patrol.

Led by Sergeant Bernie Schimmel, we scrambled down the ridge and hurriedly made our way across the airstrip toward a point near the beach where ten filled water cans awaited us. We had no cover as we made our way across the airstrip, but we reached our destination without drawing fire from the Nips. After a short rest, we prepared to make the return trip of about one mile. The filled five-gallon cans weighed about fifty pounds each, but because each can had a double handle, two men walking side by side could share the weight. We started back; each man held his rifle in one hand and the handle of a water can in the other. Sergeant Schimmel sent two men ahead to see if they would draw fire. Immediately, the sound of gunfire rang out. Neither man was hit, and we with-drew to a position of cover near the beach. We moved along the coastline toward the east until we reached a point that afforded us enough cover to make our way back to the base of the ridge.

After a short rest, we started on the last, but most difficult, leg of our journey. The ridge at that point was about sixty feet high, and the climb ahead of us was almost straight up. But by scrambling, tugging, and helping each other, we were able to reach the top. One of the men, Clarence Kanak, who was older than most of us, col-lapsed because of the exertion. The precious water was distributed to members of the company. We filled our canteens, slaked our thirsts, downed our K-rations, and prepared for another night atop the ridge.

After his promotion to division commander, General Doe made an inspection and decided that our 3rd Battalion was worn out and was losing its effectiveness. The battalion was assigned a reserve role and was directed to hold its position on the ridge. During the fight to wrest the ridge from the Nips, Company I had one man killed and six wounded.

As we watched from our position on the ridge we saw small, unarmed, single-engine Piper Cub planes taking off from and landing on the airstrip below. These planes were normally used by artillery spotters to direct our artillery fire. At this point in the fighting, however, the planes were being used in an attempt to find the exact location of the West Caves. The planes flew at very low altitudes and were often subjected to small-arms fire from the ground. We watched as they also were subjected to enemy artillery fire as they took off and landed.

As the fighting continued, it became clear that the entire area immediately north of the Mokmer airfield was honeycombed with caves that furnished the enemy with natural defensive positions. The Parai Defile had been cleared, but traffic along the coastal road was still being subjected to fire from two major pockets high on the cliffs, one near the village of Mokmer, the other near Ibdi. The major center of resistance, however, appeared to be located in a huge system of caves about 800 yards northwest of the perimeter that our company now occupied. The enemy stronghold came to be known as the West Caves, or "the sumps."

It was discovered later that the West Caves were made up of three caverns large enough to house hundreds of men. The cavern entrances were large holes in the ground varying from 75 to 125 feet in diameter. The caverns were interconnected by underground tunnels fifty to seventy-five feet below the ground. The caves occupied an area of approximately 75 x 200 yards. Included was an officers' cave, complete with houses lit with electricity supplied by gasoline generators. The officers' cave housed the headquarters of the commander of all the Japanese troops on Biak, Colonel Naoyuki Kuzume. The caves were stocked with food and ammunition. Fresh water was supplied by underground streams running through the cave complex.

After several days of fighting to clear the ridges surrounding the caves, the 1st Battalion of the 162nd Infantry took the ground controlling the cave entrances. The situation for the Japs in the sumps was hopeless, but in this kill-or-be-killed war, they had no thoughts of surrender. Our forces used tanks, flame throwers, and grenades with little effect. On June 21st, hundreds of gallons of gasoline were poured into crevices in the ground above the caves and ignited. Explosions rang out, but the Japs still controlled the entrances.

While the 1st Battalion 162nd Infantry attacked the West Caves, the 186th Infantry set up a defensive line across the road leading to the northern wilderness of Biak, thus blocking the only escape route that could be used by the Nips. During the night of June 21st, from our position on the low ridge we heard the sound of machine-gun fire coming from the direction of the West Caves. The firing continued sporadically during the night. Shortly before dawn, the sound of heavy fire rang out and continued for ten or fifteen minutes until quiet was restored.

The next morning we received the news that the 186th Infantry had killed 115 Japanese who were trying to escape to the north. Most of the Nips were killed by fire from two .50-caliber machine guns that had been set up to cover the escape route. The only man lost by the 186th Infantry was one of the machine gunners. The man was killed when a Jap jumped into his hole and exploded a grenade, killing both the GI and himself.

One of the few prisoners taken related that in the early morning hours of June 22nd, Colonel Kuzume had burned the regimental colors and all records before ordering his men to attempt an escape before morning. Hand grenades were given to the wounded so that they could destroy themselves. The prisoner said that the colonel, using his sword, then committed hara-kiri.

All opposition ended in the West Caves when the 116th Engineers lowered three 55-gallon drums of gelignite into the entrance by means of a winch and detonated them electrically. The caves were entered by the 1st Battalion 162nd Infantry on June 27th, a month to the day after our landing. Those men who entered the caves found Japanese bodies and parts of bodies throughout the caves. The troops also found evidence that cannibalism had taken place. The sight and odor were described as nauseating. It was impossible to make a reliable count of the dead, but it was estimated that about 600 men had occupied the caves.[16]

16. McCartney, *The Jungleers*, pp. 122–123.

During the assault on the West Caves by our 1st Battalion, the 34th Infantry, which had recently arrived at Biak, captured the Borokoe and Sorido airdromes against very light opposition.

After the capture of the airfields and the fall of the West Caves, General Eichelberger returned to Hollandia and General Doe took command of the task force. Only two pockets of organized enemy resistance still remained: the East Caves on the cliff north of Mokmer village and the Ibdi Pocket on an escarpment above the town of Ibdi.

The East Caves entrances, two openings about fifty feet in diameter similar to the sumps of the West Caves, were positioned on a ledge about three-quarters of the way to the top of the main ridge. The ridge at that point was almost vertical and about 200 feet high. The floor of the caves was about fifty feet below the top openings and was reached by ladders. The caves were interconnected by tunnels, and one cave had a large opening on the seaward side of the cliff from which mortars, machine guns, and 20-mm weapons were being fired.

The caves held approximately 1,000 Japanese commanded by Lieutenant Colonel Minami. The main caves were surrounded by other smaller crevices and openings on the seaward side of the cliff, all of which held enemy troops. Two observation posts on the face of the cliff gave unobstructed views of the area from Parai to the eastern end of the Mokmer drome. The openings of the cave were protected by five pillboxes built on the ridge above. Ample supplies of food and ammunition were stored in the caves.

Fire from the East Caves inflicted many casualties on our battalion on the second and third days of the campaign. On June 7th, when we made our amphibious move to Parai, we again came under fire from the caves, as did the 186th Infantry when they occupied the Mokmer airdrome. During the period from June 7th through June 23rd, the East Caves were bombarded by destroyers, tanks firing from LCTs offshore, artillery, and 4.2-inch mortars, but the fire from the caves onto the coastal road continued.

A squadron of P-40s began operations from the Mokmer drome on June 22nd. On June 24th, twelve B-25s, which had arrived the previous day, carried out what must have been the shortest bombing mission ever recorded when they skip-bombed the East Caves, which were only 1,500 yards from the airstrip. We watched from our perimeter on the ridge above the airfield as the bombers tried to hit the cave openings. The raids silenced all fire from the caves for several days. However, when engineers began working on a levee at Mokmer, harassing fire from the caves resumed and work had to be discontinued.

Artillery, tank, and 4.2-inch mortar fire on the cave area was resumed, and over 1,600 rounds were fired during the next several days. On July 3rd, in a simultaneous attack by a company of the 163rd Infantry and the 542nd Engineers, the caves were entered, and only ten Japanese were found. After Colonel Minami committed suicide on June 28th, the remaining troops evacuated the area, fleeing to the north over the ridge. After the capture of the East Caves, the only area of organized resistance remaining was the Ibdi Pocket.[17]

Although the major objectives of the Biak campaign had been achieved by July 1st, there were still many Japanese on the island. During the final phase of the capture of the East Caves, our company was occupied patrolling the area north and west of the airfields. These patrols were carried out by the entire company or, more accurately, what was left of it by that time.

We started very early one morning on one of those patrols. We moved steadily along a trail without incident for an hour or so until we neared a stream. By this time, I had become much too familiar with the odor of decomposing bodies, so I could tell by the distinctive foul scent that a decaying body was nearby. Lying face down in the shallow stream to the left of the trail was a dead Japanese soldier. As I looked at the decomposing body I wondered how many streams from which we had drunk had served as graves for the enemy. It was our normal practice to leave the dead Japanese where they had fallen, so we moved on.

Later in the morning, the first scout of our lead squad met an unwary Jap coming down the trail from the opposite direction. The Jap was dispatched quickly with a burst of bullets from the scout's tommy gun, his pockets were searched, and his gold teeth were quickly removed.

Shortly after that, while Stacy Wilson and I were the lead scouts,

17. Smith, *MacArthur's Approach*, pp. 382–383.

we spotted a hut with a thatched roof in a partial clearing about 100 yards to the right of the trail. We stopped and watched; after a moment, we saw several Japanese soldiers moving about the area. The Nips were not aware of our presence, so the CO ordered that two machine guns be set up. The guns were set in place, and the hut and the surrounding area were sprayed with fire for a short time. When no further activity was evident, Stacy and I plus three other squad members were designated to go out to the hut and investigate.

We approached carefully, staying in the jungle until we were close enough to get a clear view of the hut and the area around it. We saw two bodies lying in the clearing and upon entering found two more in the hut. The machine gunners had made our job easy; four more of the enemy had been sent to join their gods.

Among other things we found in the hut was a small suitcase completely filled with paper money. The bills were Japanese invasion currency, printed for the Dutch East Indies. The bills were worthless except for their souvenir value. We divided the contents of the suitcase into five equal portions before we returned to the rest of the company, which was waiting on the trail. Eventually, I was able to send most of the money home; I still have a small stack of those bills stashed in my closet. I have often wondered how someone in that group of Nips had accumulated such a large amount of cash; I suppose he might have been a paymaster.

We had no other contacts with the enemy as we continued along the trail until early afternoon. Then we reversed our direction and started the return hike to our perimeter. During the long march back that afternoon, the three members of our squad's BAR team, Smitty, Sal, and Johns, started to argue about whose turn it was to carry the BAR. Because the BAR weighed nineteen pounds as compared to the six pounds of the carbines carried by the other two members of the team, it was normal procedure for the men to take turns carrying the BAR and the ammunition needed for it.

It was not unusual for the three men to argue; they were much like three brothers who often bickered before settling their disputes. But on that hot afternoon, the argument continued until Charles Johns, who was carrying the BAR at the time, announced that if neither of the other men would carry the heavy weapon, neither would he. With that pronouncement, he put the BAR down alongside the trail and moved on without a weapon. It was only a matter of seconds until our assistant squad leader, John Stallons, who was at the rear of our squad, found the weapon on the ground. The sergeant, a large muscular man, quickly and none too gently settled the dispute. We heard no more from the BAR team that afternoon.

Later that afternoon, our lead scout noticed movement in the jungle near the trail. Rather than fire, he held up and waited. Soon, two GIs with cameras came out onto the path. The two men, members of the hospital staff, were looking for orchids to photograph. They were told that they were lucky not to have been killed and were advised to get back to the hospital and stay there. The men said that they had no idea that there were still Japs in the area; they sheepishly agreed to return to their base and remain close to it.

I don't know how many miles we covered that day, but I am certain it was the longest march we ever made during my time in the Southwest Pacific. Most of us were not in very good condition after six continuous weeks of hard combat. The trail was very muddy, and the weather was steamy and hot. By the time we reached our perimeter just before dusk I was exhausted. I think we must have hiked about twenty miles that day.

During the first week of July, we received the welcome news that we would leave our perimeter and move to an area near the ocean where a field hospital had been set up. We made the move that day and set up a perimeter around the hospital. For all practical purposes, that was the end of the Biak campaign for our company. That evening I wrote to my mother, "We have had a second round with Tojo's boys and I was fortunate again. I didn't even get a little scratch. I'd forgotten that this was the 4th of July. I won't miss the fireworks though; I've seen enough for awhile."

One of the benefits of our move to the beach was that we were able to bathe in the ocean. Other than being soaked by the almost daily rain showers, we had not bathed since we landed on Biak. Another morale booster was the fact that we finally started to receive a lot of back mail; one day I received forty-four letters. One was a birthday letter. It had been on the way for three and a half months. I also received a couple of packages that had been sent three months earlier. Almost everything was smashed or ruined. One box contained chocolate candies with the individual brown wrappers sticking up out of the melted chocolate. In a letter of thanks to Kay, I wrote, "Those were the best chocolate-covered wrappers I've ever eaten." I had asked my folks to send me a small metal mirror; when it arrived it was already rusted. The salt air of the ocean and the humidity of the jungle played havoc with most materials.

Although we were still sleeping on the ground and performing guard duty at night, the almost nightly bombing raids by Washing-Machine Charlie were the only real danger. An outdoor movie screen had been set up at the hospital, and we were allowed to attend when we were not on guard duty. Quite regularly, the movies were interrupted by bombing raids, often by a lone Japanese bomber.

During our short stay near the hospital, I set up an aquarium on the lip of our foxhole. A coral shelf extended several hundred yards from the shoreline near our perimeter, and at low tide this shelf was uncovered. On the shelf a number of small pools had been created by bombs that had exploded and formed depressions in the coral. When the tide went out, small colorful tropical fish were often trapped in those pools. Using our fatigue caps as nets, Stacy and I caught enough fish to stock the aquarium, a large, white, porcelain-coated bowl that I found in a nearby hut. To keep the fish alive I added fresh seawater each morning. I feel safe in saying that we had the only foxhole in the Southwest Pacific furnished with an aquarium.

During the daylight hours, we spent most of the time resting in our foxholes. We used our ponchos to make tent-like covers over the holes. The ponchos sheltered us from the scorching rays of the equatorial sun. In the early morning hours, many of us walked along the beach gathering beautiful seashells that we sent home to our mothers, sisters, wives, or sweethearts.

I don't remember seeing any natives at Hollandia, nor had I seen any at Biak until we set up our perimeter near the hospital. Because most of the shooting had ended, the natives, usually referred to as Gooks or Fuzzy Wuzzies, were beginning to come out of the jungle. Most of the men and children wore loincloths or shorts. Most of the women were dressed in what could best be described as sarongs, but some wore only skirts. No one wore shoes. How they could walk without shoes on that sharp coral was difficult to understand, but going barefoot did not seem to bother them. One day we watched barefoot young boys playing soccer using a ball carved from the wood of a coconut tree.

Many of the natives chewed betel nut, the seed of the betel palm tree. The juices caused their lips to redden. The combination of the bright red lips and very black skin made an unforgettable sight, particularly when the person broke into a broad smile. Most of the native men were quite friendly and would ask for cigarettes. Even boys as young as six or seven would smoke if we gave them cigarettes. Most of the women were shy and kept to themselves. I suspect that the natives may have prudently accepted the Japanese when they controlled the island; however, those natives we saw seemed genuinely happy to have us in charge.

After a few weeks, the attire of many of the natives, especially the children, changed dramatically. We saw children wearing army or navy caps, undershirts, neckties, and even sunglasses, all donated by soldiers or sailors. We marveled at the ease with which they could climb the tall branchless trunks of the coconut palms to get coconuts for us. Often they asked for cigarettes as a reward for their efforts. Usually, someone who did not smoke would supply the cigarettes. The only other way we could obtain coconuts was by ramming the tree trunk with a Sherman tank. The tanks were not usually available for such duty, so we relied on the natives to get those treats for us. I did see a few GIs try to scale those trees, but their efforts invariably met with failure. The only crops other than coconuts that I ever saw growing were sweet potatoes and sugar cane. The principal item of food was fish. Birds and wild pigs were other sources of meat.

One afternoon as I sat near the shore, I watched a young boy repeatedly diving into the ocean. He would stay submerged for what seemed like inordinately long periods, come up for air, and dive again. After at least twelve or fifteen dives, he emerged holding his arm over his head. Attached to his wrist was a small octopus that he had at last pried loose from the ocean bottom. He then had the problem of getting the octopus off his arm. After several minutes he succeeded, then killed the creature by hitting it against a rock. Carrying his prize, he went happily on his way.

Some of the natives used outrigger canoes and nets to take their catches. I presume that most of them had lived in the thatched huts that were usually built on stilts offshore. Apparently most of them had been dispossessed by the Japs, because we found Japanese articles in almost all the huts. One day a family, led by a man carrying his long fishing spear, came out of the jungle. He was followed by five or six children and, at the end of the line, a woman carrying a huge bundle on her back. I'm certain that the bundle contained all their worldly possessions.

Dutch missionaries had at one time operated a school at Biak, and some of the natives could speak pidgin English, a mixture of English and the native language. Every GI was "Joe" to the natives. One day several of us were talking to a young man, and he asked us if we wanted a "sing song." When we replied "yes" he started to sing "Shoo Shoo Baby." After being rewarded with enthusiastic applause he smiled broadly and broke into his version of "My Darling Clementine." He liked performing as much as we enjoyed listening to him. I had heard stories about the cannibals of some sections of New Guinea, but the people of Biak seemed to be a peaceful and happy community.

On another occasion, while I was talking to a young lad who spoke English fairly well, I showed my rosary to him. He knew what it was and asked me to give it to him. I turned him down because I thought that I might have a greater need for it than he. I knew that his life expectancy as a native of Biak was only thirty-five to forty years; I was using my rosary to pray that my life expectancy would equal or surpass his.

Although the fighting had ended for our company, Japanese resistance still continued at the Ibdi Pocket. Initial attacks on the pocket of resistance, located high on the ridge overlooking the village of Ibdi, were carried out by the 2nd Battalion of the 162nd Infantry on June 1st. Attacks continued until June 7th, when our 3rd Battalion bypassed the Parai Defile by making an amphibious landing west of the defile. Attacks on the Ibdi Pocket were then suspended to concentrate efforts on clearing the Parai Defile by attacks from both the west and the east.

On June 21st, the 2nd Battalion of the 163rd Infantry renewed operations to clear the Ibdi Pocket. From June 21st through June 25th, the area was bombarded by artillery and mortars. Over the next three days, the 1st and 2nd Battalions of the 163rd Infantry attacked the pocket, making some progress, but on June 29th, the infantry attacks were halted and the bombardment of the area was resumed. During the period from July 4th through July 7th, the 146th Artillery fired 5,500 rounds and the 163rd Infantry fired 2,400 mortar shells into the pocket area, but Japanese resistance continued.

On July 9th, the artillery and mortar bombardments were resumed, and P-39s and P-40s dive-bombed and strafed the area. From June 21st through July 10th, the 146th Artillery fired about twenty thousand 105-mm shells into the area, and the 163rd Infantry fired at least that many mortar rounds on the enemy. The jungle surrounding the caves and pillboxes was almost cleared by the bombardment; although the size of the pocket had been reduced, the Nips refused to surrender.

On July 12th, howitzers of the 947th Artillery and tanks were brought up to fire on the area, and on July 13th about 200 Japs fled across the ridge to the north, but some resistance still continued. During the period from July 10th through July 20th, another 6,000 artillery shells were fired into the pocket. On July 22nd, B-24 Liberators dropped sixty-four 1,000-pound bombs on the enemy. Following another artillery and mortar bombardment of about 2,000 rounds, the 163rd Infantry moved into the area and found all organized resistance had ended. Mopping up continued until July 28th, when the last enemy resistance was wiped out.

When our troops examined the pocket after the fighting had ended, they found that the central part of the pocket covered an area of about 400 by 600 yards. The area contained four large and seventeen smaller caves, surrounded by seventy-five log-and-coral pillboxes, each large enough to hold four men. The large caves were used as living quarters and aid stations, and originally housed about 1,000 Japanese. Weapons included 37-mm and 75-mm artillery, heavy and light mortars, 20-mm guns, light and heavy machine guns, and varied small arms.[18]

Many words could be used to describe the Japanese defense of the Ibdi Pocket, but the two words that I feel best describe the fight that took place are maniacal and fanatical. As an infantryman, nothing was more discouraging to me than to watch the enemy

18. Smith, *MacArthur's Approach,* pp. 388–390.

being bombarded unmercifully until I was certain that no one could have survived, then to begin an attack and find that, incredibly, we were still under fire from Nips in a pillbox, cave, or foxhole. The fact that almost all the Japanese fighting men preferred to die rather than surrender made our war a series of difficult, savage, and merciless encounters.

The reduction of the Ibdi Pocket also illustrated the willingness of our officers to expend unbelievable amounts of ammunition to destroy enemy installations and thereby save the lives of many infantrymen, who were eventually called upon to attack and subdue the enemy.

Our officers received criticism for lack of aggressiveness during the Biak campaign, but certainly the schedule for the capture of Biak and its airfields was not realistic and was based on faulty intelligence about the number of Japanese on the island. The accepted rules of warfare call for an attacking force to have a numerical advantage of three to one in troop strength. The number of U.S. troops in the original HURRICANE Task Force approximately equaled the number of the Japanese who were defending Biak and who had the advantages of the extraordinary terrain on their side.

When the Biak campaign was being planned, MacArthur's G-2 (Military Intelligence) Officer, General Charles Willoughby, estimated that the Japanese forces on Biak numbered between 4,400 and 5,000 troops. In fact, the island was defended by 12,350 Japanese. It is thought that about 1,200 enemy reinforcements came ashore after our landing. Those troops were brought to Biak by barge from Noemfoor and were landed on the north coast at Korim Bay. Most of the Japs on Biak were killed or destroyed themselves; some undoubtedly fled to the farther reaches of the island, where many died of starvation. A total of only thirteen Japanese had been taken prisoner when organized resistance ended. Only one of the thirteen was a combat soldier. Other Japanese surrendered singly or in small groups after the fighting ended. The final count of prisoners taken was 220. U.S. casualties are listed as 474 killed, 2,443 wounded, and 7,234 nonbattle casualties. The nonbattle casualties resulted from malaria, hepatitis, scrub typhus, dengue fever, psychoneurosis, and other afflictions. Total casualties numbered 10,151, approximately equaling the number of U.S.

troops making the original landings. The victory at Biak had not come cheaply.[19]

In a letter written to members of the 41st Division at the conclusion of the Biak campaign General Doe described the contributions of the various branches of the division during the fight for Biak. In assessing the role of the infantry, General Doe wrote:

> No other task in the Division is comparable to the load carried by the infantry soldier. He is our only reason for existence. He is the man who captures and holds the ground. He carries the fight to the enemy. The infantry soldier was the one who met in hand-to-hand combat the crack troops of the Japanese, threw him from his positions, destroyed him, and gave us our victory. To these men we are eternally grateful and a pride rises in our hearts that is going to carry us on from victory to victory in the future.[20]

19. Smith, *MacArthur's Approach,* pp. 392, 577.
20. McCartney, *The Jungleers,* p. 184. Quote in McCartney.

Author at Camp Roberts, summer 1943.

Troops of the 163rd Infantry landing on Wakde Island, New Guinea, May 18, 1944. From McCartney, *The Jungleers*.

Members of the 41st Division aboard ship.

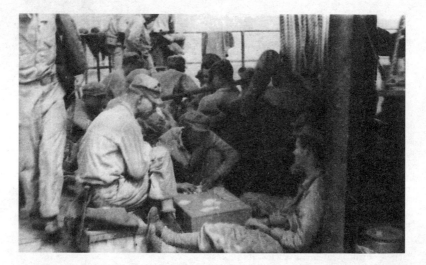

New Guinea coastline (near Hollandia).

Troops of the 163rd Infantry under fire on beach of Wakde Island, New Guinea, May 18, 1944. From McCartney, *The Jungleers.*

Members of 105-mm artillery team in action at Sarmi, New Guinea, May 1944. *The Saturday Evening Post,* July 27, 1946.

LCIs carrying troops of 41st Division for landing at Biak on May 27, 1944. From McCartney, *The Jungleers.*

New Guinea natives.

Japanese tanks destroyed in the first tank battle of the Pacific War at Biak on May 29, 1944.

Author shoveling coral to be used as tent floor at Biak, July 1944.

Members of Company I 162nd Infantry and 3rd Battalion Commander Paul Hollister prepare to attack cave on Biak, June 1944. Those identifiable (*left to right closest to cave*): Paul Hollister, Les Perry, George Cooley, Orville Alexander. From McCartney, *The Jungleers.*

Troops of the 41st Division wade through swamp on Biak, June 1944. *The Saturday Evening Post,* September 3, 1949.

Troops of the 41st Division accompanied by Sherman tank, Biak, June 1944. From Smith, *The Approach to the Philippines.*

Members of heavy weapons company firing mortars on Biak, June 1944. From McCartney, *The Jungleers.*

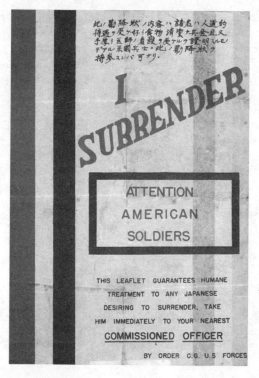

比ノ勸降狀ノ内容ハ諸君ハ人道的
待遇ヲ受ケ好イ食物 清實ナ兵食且又
手厚キ医師ノ看護ヲ受ケルヲ證明スルモ
デアル米國兵士ニ比ノ勸降狀ヲ
携帶スレバ可ナリ.

I
SURRENDER®

ATTENTION
AMERICAN
SOLDIERS

THIS LEAFLET GUARANTEES HUMANE
TREATMENT TO ANY JAPANESE
DESIRING TO SURRENDER. TAKE
HIM IMMEDIATELY TO YOUR NEAREST
COMMISSIONED OFFICER

BY ORDER C.G. U.S FORCES

Surrender leaflet dropped by U.S. planes on Biak, June 1944.

Japanese prisoner taken at Hollandia, April 1944.

Christmas card designed by member of the 41st Division for Christmas 1944. The name "41st Division Butchers" was originated by Tokyo Rose.

Infantrymen accompanied by Sherman tank enlarge beachhead at Zamboanga, Philippines, March 1945. From McCartney, *The Jungleers.*

Troops of the 41st Division under fire, Davao, Mindanao area, June 1945. From McCartney, *The Jungleers.*

Author at camp in
Zamboanga, Phil-
ippines, summer
1945.

Author at Japa-
nese seaplane
base, Fukuyama,
Japan, autumn
1945.

Photo of ruins of Hiroshima taken by author, October 1945.

5

A Welcome Respite

After the fall of the Ibdi Pocket, only scattered resistance remained in the northern part of the island, so it was no longer necessary for our company to guard the hospital. We moved to an area east of the Mokmer airstrip and began to set up camp. However, we had barely completed pitching the tents when a snafu was discovered; the air force wanted to use the area as a camp for members of its ground crew. The fact that we had to defer to the air force did not please us. Despite much bitching, we moved to an area farther from the airstrip and began to set up camp for the second time.

We pitched about thirty tents, enough to house all the members of the company when it would reach full strength again. The tents were set up in two rows, leaving enough space between the rows for the company street. At the end of the street, tents were pitched for the officers, the company headquarters, and the supply room. A kitchen tent was set up, and a Lister bag filled with clean drinking water was hung outside. Large coconut logs were placed around the perimeter of each tent, and crushed coral was hauled in to form a raised floor that would stay dry during heavy rains. We used smaller logs to build racks to hang our mess kits outside our tents. Best of all, we received the old standby army cots. We built wooden racks above the cots, on which we hung mosquito netting. We dug a latrine and set up several 55-gallon drums on stilts to serve as showers. We were going to live in relative luxury.

As we settled in at our rest camp northeast of the Mokmer airstrip, our barracks bags containing clean clothes and personal items were brought to us. We were able to change to clean clothes for the first time in almost three months. One of the men in the company volunteered to serve as the company barber, and for one guilder, about fifty cents, I received my first haircut since leaving Australia four months earlier. Copies of the *Front Lines,* a daily news bulletin published by division headquarters, were posted on a bulletin board outside the company headquarters tent. We read about the favorable progress of the war both in the Pacific and in Europe. Mail began to arrive more promptly, sometimes in as little as two weeks. Sunday church services were held in a chapel that had been built with coconut logs, and movies were shown on a large outdoor screen. On most nights, the movies were interrupted by air-raid alerts and on some nights by actual bombing attacks. Those raids were often carried out by a single Japanese plane and were mostly of nuisance value to the enemy. One night, a movie I particularly wanted to see was interrupted five times by air-raid alerts.

Three and a half months had passed since we had left Finschhafen to make the Hollandia landing. We had existed solely on K-rations and slept on the ground the entire time. Most of the men still with the company were suffering with dysentery, jungle rot, or other afflictions. At Biak, we had been in constant contact with the enemy during the entire campaign. Living day and night for such an extended period under the conditions of combat caused anxiety and a feeling of near exhaustion. Most of us were near the breaking point when the fighting came to an end.

I don't know what the company strength was as we set up our camp, but I am certain that there were fewer than half of the original 180 men. My best estimate would be that about seventy men were still with the company. I do know that Del Cochran and I were the only men in my original squad of twelve who made it through the entire Biak campaign. Of the thirty-nine men in our platoon who made the landing, only fifteen were still with the company when the fighting ended.

One day, shortly after we set up camp, there was a call for everyone suffering with jungle rot. Most of the company fell out naked into the company street, where the medics went from man to man painting the infected areas with big cotton swabs soaked in potassium permanganate solution. Jungle rot occurred most commonly under arms or between legs, but it could occur on any skin area, including the face. The medication left bright purple stains on the skin. After the medics completed their disagreeable task, we patients, or "paintees," were a sorrowful but colorful and ludicrous sight.

Throughout most of our battles in the Southwest Pacific, the company served as the basic unit. We seldom ventured far afield in smaller numbers, and although our movements were coordinated with those of the other companies of our battalion, most of the time the company operated as a separate unit. Our nightly perimeters were almost always made up exclusively of men from our company. There were no front lines, only scattered perimeters in the jungle. At night, the enemy roamed freely between and around those perimeters.

The company was the family; the platoon, the close relatives; and the squad, the immediate family. In our immediate family, I developed a close relationship with several men. Stacy Wilson, a farm boy from Greasy Ridge, Ohio, was first scout in our squad. As second scout, I followed in his footsteps along the jungle trails on Biak. He projected a carefree appearance as he moved out as first scout, often carrying his rifle at an angle over his shoulder as if he were squirrel-hunting in the woods of Ohio. He was a likeable, easy-going GI. Stacy's height and build were about the same as mine; neither of us presented a very big target for the Nips.

Ed Janaskie, a large, strong man of Polish descent, was a coal miner from Shamokin, Pennsylvania. The thing I remember most about Ed was the way in which he attacked the hard coral soil on Biak as we attempted to dig our foxhole each night. He would often order me to get out of his way so that he could wield one of the miniature shovels or picks that each of us carried. Ed would usually remove his fatigue jacket while he dug, and the sweat would run down his face and bare chest. I remember one afternoon when Ed, his uniform soaked with perspiration, was following me as we moved up a trail. Exasperated, he said, "Damn you, Zero! How can a little guy like you carry all that stuff and not even work up a sweat?"

Arthur Smith and Sal Ferrara, both members of the BAR team in our squad, were from the big city, New York. Smitty, called Ack Ack by some of the men, lived in Queens. Sal's home was in Brooklyn. Smitty, about my height but of a somewhat stockier build, was an outgoing, enthusiastic GI who could find humor in almost any situation. Sal also had a good sense of humor, but he was not as exuberant as Smitty. Sal, of Italian descent, was a rather large man with an ample Roman nose. All of us had joined Company I as replacements in Rockhampton. Stacy, Smitty, and Sal were about my age. Ed was probably in his mid-twenties. Ed became the last casualty in our company at Biak when he was seriously wounded by mortar fire while we fought on the ridge overlooking the airstrip. Sal was wounded later at Zamboanga. Sal returned to the company after recovering from his wound, but we never saw or heard about Ed again. We usually learned if a wounded man had died, but we never heard, at least at my level, how seriously the others had been wounded.

When I think about men who were wounded and never returned to the company, the name of Sergeant Glennon Stanek comes to mind. He was an assistant squad leader in our platoon. He was a well-built, handsome man with wavy blond hair. But it was not just his good looks that caused him to stand out in my memory; it was the fact that he always looked cleaner and neater than the rest of us. It seemed that he was always clean shaven while most of us wore shaggy, dirty beards. I hated shaving with rusty, dull razor blades and brushless shaving cream, but I also hated the itchy, dirty feeling of my beard, so I shaved whenever I felt that I had enough water or when I couldn't stand the beard any longer. Sergeant Stanek often used some of his precious water supply to shave and even brush his teeth. How he could slog through the mud and sleep on the ground and still look so clean was beyond my understanding. Sergeant Stanek was wounded on the second day at Biak by shrapnel that tore into his back and legs. As he was carried out, I wondered if he could survive what appeared to be a very serious wound. It did not seem right that such a handsome, able man should be struck down by an enemy mortar shell. He did survive, but he never returned to the company.

Almost fifty years later, I still retain vivid memories of Biak and the fighting that took place there. Probably the most surprising and discouraging thing was the fact that we seldom saw the enemy. The Japs, for the most part, were willing to watch our movements from their positions on the high ground and then pound us with mortar fire or to wait in their caves and pillboxes until we came into their line of fire. It was rare for us to see a Nip in the open and be able to fire the first shot. Most of the time we returned fire into the jungle at the unseen enemy. I have often read about the way that Jap snipers camouflaged themselves in trees, but during the many days of combat in which I took part, I never saw a Jap in a tree or thought that I was being fired on by a sniper hidden in one.

I remember the frightening but thrilling feeling of following Stacy along a jungle trail as a scout, fearing what might be awaiting us around each bend in the trail. My chance for survival, I reasoned, depended partially on my ability to spot the enemy before he saw me. I knew, of course, that if the enemy were dug in or lying in wait, the chances of that happening were slim at best.

It was a very different feeling, however, to be subjected to mortar fire. It was the experience that frightened me most. To hear the sound of the mortar firing and to know that the shells were arching silently through the air toward us always made me feel not only frightened but vulnerable and helpless. It was at those times that I wished that my steel helmet were large enough to cover my whole body. No matter how hard I pulled it down, though, it only covered part of my head. I can still recall the sound of those Japanese mortars as they were fired, the seconds of silence as the shells traveled toward us, the sound of the explosion as the shells hit the ground, and the calls of "Medic!" that much too often rang out immediately afterward.

Looking back, I think that Company I fared better than many of the others. In our battalion, Company K was hit particularly hard. Our company suffered many casualties, but relatively few men were killed. The normal ratio of wounded to killed was about three and a half or four to one. During the Biak campaign, eight members of Company I were killed; forty were wounded. Nonbattle casualties probably numbered sixty-five to seventy men.

Among those nonbattle casualties were what we called psycho cases; the medical term was psychoneurosis or psychiatric breakdown. I saw men who reached a point where they could not endure the carnage around them and involuntarily lost control. Some would shake violently, others would not or could not respond, and some would just sit and stare silently. Most of the men who became psycho casualties never returned to the company.

U.S. Army records show that about 15 percent of all casualties during World War II were psychiatric casualties. The records show that as the number of days of combat increased, the number of psychiatric casualties increased dramatically. That fact was borne out at Biak. Many of our psycho casualties were veterans of the Papuan campaign. Studies indicate that the useful life of a combat soldier was limited. Almost every man could be expected to break down at some point.

There was one man in our platoon who had no problems whatsoever during the daylight hours but fell apart at night. One night at Biak, he was assigned to my foxhole. On his first watch, I was awakened by rapid rifle fire from our hole. When I sat up, I saw that the man was shaking violently. He said, "There are Japs out there." I reached for my M1 but it was not at my side, where I had put it before falling asleep. After a few seconds of panic, I realized that our nervous buddy, after emptying his rifle, had grabbed my M1 and fired a second clip at "those Japs." There were no dead Japs to be found the next morning, but I had a rifle that needed cleaning. Shortly after that, the man left the company as a psychiatric casualty.

I had sympathy for that GI because I personally found the nights difficult. The grind of being on guard for three one-hour periods each night was very tiring. It would seem to have been better for each man to take one three-hour watch each night, but I don't think any of us could have stayed awake that long; I know for certain that I would have fallen asleep. Often during those one-hour guard periods, I would stick my finger into my canteen and put a few drops of water in my eyes to keep myself awake. Despite the fact that each dawn announced the beginning of another day of combat, I was always happy when the night had come to an end.

The tension of the nights was heightened by the utter darkness of the jungle. On most nights we were under a dense canopy of trees; there was almost total blackness, even on clear, moonlit nights. It was easy to become disoriented under those conditions. One dark night, I finished my watch and woke the man next to me. I had lain down and was ready to go to sleep when a feeling came over me that something was wrong. I sat up and found that the man on watch was facing toward the next hole rather than toward the outside of the perimeter. We had strung ponchos over our hole that night and he was staring at the poncho, which was only a few inches from his face. A man in another company in our battalion was accidentally killed one night when a GI in the hole next to him became disoriented and fired into the neighboring foxhole.

The sounds of the jungle night were another unnerving factor. The wind in the trees, the movement of wildlife, or the calls of birds could stir the imagination. There were any number of sounds that could be interpreted as an enemy moving through the jungle or sending signals to his cohorts. Of course, the tossing of a grenade or the firing of a rifle by a member of the perimeter would usually wake most of us. I do remember, though, times when I was so tired that I would not even bother to sit up when that happened. On most nights, I was not much concerned about a banzai attack because our perimeters were usually set up in areas with such heavy undergrowth that it would not have been possible for large numbers of the enemy to make a charge through the jungle. I was more concerned about small groups of Nips who might be trying to infiltrate our perimeters.

The Japanese used the nights to patrol, to attack, or to move to new positions. A favorite nighttime tactic of the Japs was to find and cut our telephone wires and then wait in ambush for our repair crews to arrive the next morning.

Our offensive moves were always made during the daylight hours. The nights were the time to defend our perimeters and get as much sleep as the situation allowed. I approved wholeheartedly of that SOP. Prowling through the jungle in the pitch-black darkness in search of the Japs made no sense at all to me. I much preferred to spend the nights in a foxhole and let the Nips try to find us. After we had dug in for the night, we tried to make ourselves as inconspicuous as possible. We never left our holes for any reason. We never fired our weapons or threw grenades unless we were reasonably certain that the Nips were near. Oftentimes, they were probably much closer than we thought.

One night early in the fight for Biak, I was sitting in our hole serving the last watch of the night. Whenever I was given a choice, I would opt to take the last watch. Even as a young man I had adopted an early-to-bed and early-to-rise routine. On that morning, as dawn began to break, I could see that there was something on the ground near the foxhole next to ours. As the light slowly improved,

I was able to determine what it was: a Japanese rifle with fixed bayonet. The point of the bayonet was about six feet from the edge of the adjacent foxhole. The owner of the rifle was nowhere in sight. Apparently, he had been wounded and crawled away, leaving his rifle behind.

The stress of the fighting, seeing buddies wounded and killed, and trying to survive under such severe conditions caused men to react in different ways. A self-inflicted gun wound was one of the less courageous ways. The favorite method was to shoot oneself in the foot. Usually the culprit would claim that the gun fired accidentally, but others admitted that their action was taken to avoid further combat. A man in Company L was so distraught that he fired a bullet into his head, killing himself. One man in our company went so far as to remove his shoe and sock before shooting himself so that the medics could treat him quickly. Another man tried three times to shoot his foot, but he always flinched at the last second and missed. In an attempt to stop the practice, Division Headquarters issued a pronouncement that any self-inflicted wound would be treated as a court-martial offense. Not only the perpetrator of the act but anyone in his presence when the shooting took place would be subject to court-martial. I suppose that some of those who shot themselves were psycho cases, but I believe that most of the men who did so were just looking for an "easy" way out.

The great majority of the men in our outfit did what had to be done. All of us, I am sure, were frightened at times. If there were any who were not, they were most unusual men. The reasons why we persevered were probably similar. An incident took place one day that helped me decide what my obligations were and why I should carry them out.

Early in the Biak campaign, we were moving up a jungle trail when a man a short distance ahead of me collapsed and fell to the ground. The medics examined him, then picked him up, put him on a stretcher, and carried him back to the field hospital. As we started up the trail again, the thought flashed across my mind that if I were to fall down and say that I was in great pain, I too could go back to the relative safety of the hospital. As we continued our advance, I looked around at my comrades who were doggedly plodding along, and I realized immediately that to do such a thing would be to take the coward's way out. It would not have been fair to the other men. As I continued to think about the subject, I looked at those men again. Some of them were stronger, more able soldiers than I, but most of them were rather ordinary young men. If they could stick it out, I thought, so could I. Personal pride and a sense of duty were the motivating factors for me to carry on and do whatever had to be done.

The term "typical GI" was used to describe soldiers in stories written during the war. I would have a difficult time in picking out a typical GI in our company. There were men in their teens, twenties, thirties, and even forties. Most of the men were single, but some were married, and a few were fathers. There were men from large cities: New York, Philadelphia, Chicago, Los Angeles, Detroit, St. Louis, and most other large towns. There were men from small towns with names such as Thrall, Texas; La Moure, North Dakota; Jarvis Store, Kentucky; Spring Creek, Tennessee; Powell Butte, Oregon; and many others.

Most of the men had high school educations, two were college graduates, and there was one man in our platoon who could neither read nor write. There were men who had no idea where New Guinea was, nor did they have any interest in finding out.

Almost all of us could trace our ancestry to the European countries. The U.S. Army was segregated in those days, so there were no black men in our outfit. The only black soldiers I ever saw were those men who served as coxswains on the DUKWs that carried the fourth and fifth waves ashore at Biak. Nisei (persons born in America of parents who emigrated from Japan) were also segregated, and most served in the European Theater. Exceptions were those Nisei who served in the Pacific Theater as interpreters to question the few prisoners who were taken and to translate any enemy documents recovered. I don't remember any other Orientals in our outfit. Religious backgrounds also varied widely. The one thread that tied us together was the job to be done. Most of us knew that unless we were wounded, became seriously ill, or were killed, we would be somewhere in the Pacific Theater until the war had come to an end.

One thing that I learned about Japanese soldiers during the Hollandia and Biak campaigns was that there were major differences between their support troops and their combat infantrymen.

At Hollandia, we faced mostly service and supply units; the line or infantry units of the Japanese 18th Army had moved to Wewak to defend against the expected landing there. Most of the support troops left behind did not fight; many of them fled. Many who did not flee surrendered.

At Biak, we were opposed by soldiers of the Japanese 222nd Infantry and a company of the 36th Division tanks, veterans of campaigns in China and Burma. These troops were reinforced by 1,500 naval troops, field artillery, and anti-aircraft units, as well as a detachment of marines, all of whom were at least six feet tall. Soldiers of the 36th Division had a reputation throughout the Orient for their cruelty. After the fighting on Biak came to an end, an order was found that called for the beheading of any U.S. troops taken prisoner.

The Japanese troops on Biak fought stubbornly and well, at times even fanatically. When their situation became hopeless, the overwhelming majority still would not surrender. They either continued to fight until killed or they destroyed themselves. The typical example of this behavior was demonstrated at the West Caves, when Colonel Kuzume, before disemboweling himself with his sword, issued hand grenades to all the wounded so that they could kill themselves rather than suffer the shame of surrendering. We knew nothing about the order of the Japanese samurai or the Bushido code, but I believe that most of us who took part in those fierce battles would grudgingly confess to some admiration for the dedication of the Japanese fighting man to his ideals and for his willingness, in some instances eagerness, to give his life for them.

The following entry in a diary found in the West Caves and published in the *Front Lines* describes the feelings of one Japanese soldier trapped in the cave:

> Under existing conditions we are helpless. Let us be guardian Spirits of the Empire. There were about 30 wounded soldiers left in the cave; those who could move assisted the others. They all shouted "Long live our Emperor" before leaving this world. My friend Nagasaka stabbed his throat with a knife, but did not succeed in killing himself. I finally decided to assist him so that he could rest in peace. I stabbed my own brother in arms. Who could understand my horrible predicament? I still have two grenades; one to destroy myself and one for the enemy. I don't know whether or not my rations will last until we are rescued.

I am determined to kill myself before I lose the power to pull the grenade pin. I want to restore my health so that I can die on the battlefield and follow Nagasaka. Long live the Emperor! Father and Mother, please forgive me for dying before you do. I hope that you will be able to live the rest of your lives in peace. I wish you good health. I have done my duty to my country. My dearest parents, I am committing suicide with a hand grenade. My ashes will not reach you.[1]

In an effort to encourage the Japanese to surrender, leaflets guaranteeing humane treatment to those who did so were dropped from our aircraft onto areas occupied by the Japanese. The leaflets, which were printed in English and Japanese, contained a drawing depicting a Japanese soldier in a tattered uniform alone on an island surrounded by the ocean. Because we never saw a Jap surrender on Biak either with or without a leaflet, Smitty maintained that the only thing we were accomplishing by dropping the leaflets was furnishing the Nips with toilet paper.

When writing about his experiences in the Southwest Pacific, General Eichelberger said that he had never seen terrain more difficult than that of Biak, a coral island covered with rain forest and jungle undergrowth and pockmarked with caves. Those of us who fought there would agree that the terrain was difficult for us, the attackers, but it was certainly an asset for the defenders. The numerous caves and caverns furnished the enemy with natural defensive positions. The hard coral of the island made our attempts to dig in for the nights extremely difficult, and in some places impossible. On those nights when we could not dig in, we gathered large pieces of coral and piled them around us for protection. Mosquitoes, flies, gnats, and many other insects flourished. We shared our foxholes with snakes, lizards, and other crawling creatures. The days were hot and steamy; rain showers were numerous.

Most of the water on Biak came from underground streams. Water fit to drink was always in short supply, and its taste and odor could best be described as foul. The Halazone pills that we used for water purification did nothing to make the taste more palatable. The directions for the use of the Halazone, a chlorine compound, re-

---

1. Kahn, *Between Tedium and Terror,* pp. 155–56.

quired a waiting period of thirty minutes after addition of the pills before drinking the water. Because water was so difficult to find on Biak and because we usually did not stop that long at the few streams we could find, many of us filled our canteens, dropped in the tablets, and proceeded to drink the water immediately or shortly after that. Then we would refill our canteens. Following that procedure allowed us to quench our thirsts and leave with full canteens.

At Hollandia, I learned that I could survive fairly well with little or no food, but, particularly in those extremely hot jungles, water was an absolute necessity. One night at Biak when we needed water, I used my helmet to collect runoff rainwater from ponchos strung over our foxhole. When I tasted it the next morning, I was terribly disappointed. The rainwater tasted as bad as the rest of the water on Biak.

Sleeping on the hard coral was not only uncomfortable but it often caused circulation problems for me, particularly in my arms. I often woke to find that I had no feeling in one of my arms because it had been pressed against a rock or a root that cut off circulation. When this happened I would use my "good" arm to feel in the dark to locate the other arm, then begin to massage it until the feeling in it returned.

Imagine my dismay one night to awaken and find that both of my arms were numb. I could not move either arm. After some effort, I found that I could move the fingers on one hand. I began to open and close the fingers until gradually the feeling began to return to the whole arm. When I was able to move that arm I felt around for the other arm and massaged it until the feeling returned and I was able to move both arms again.

We often slept in the rain, and I remember one night when our shallow foxhole filled with runoff water. We spent the night trying to sleep while sitting on our steel helmets. Usually when we dug our foxholes, we tried to pile the dirt and coral around the holes so that any runoff water would be directed away from our "home for the night," but on that particular night our efforts had been in vain. I always slept with my boots on when we were in combat; it gave me a feeling of security. I felt that I would be ready for any eventuality. On that rainy night, however, my boots suffered because of that practice. My thoughts went back to basic training where we had been instructed to wear a clean pair of socks each day and to alternate our boots every day in order to maintain healthy feet.

I have been able to find only a handful of articles about Biak and the campaign we fought there. My favorite description of Biak and its people is the one in a poem written by John J. Bick, Flight Officer, ATC. The poem that follows appeared in the *St. Louis Post-Dispatch* in 1944.

When Kipling wrote of Mandalay
And flying fish and stuff,
Of elephants and teakwood and
Of living that is rough,
He might have known his India
But on my word—sad sack—
He never saw this hopeless place—
The Island of Biak.

O yes, we have the palm trees and
The coconuts galore,
The lovely blue Pacific too,
To wash the coral shore,
And natives by the score or so
Each in his filthy shack,
But for the life of me, the Dutch
Can have Biak.

I've dipped into the salty surf,
I've wandered on the shore,
I've seen the golden sunset when
The blist'ring day was o'er;
I've tasted of the tropics, but
There's something that they lack
I have no hopes of finding on
The Island of Biak.

I've seen the South Sea movies of
Slim girls in gay sarongs,
Who danced in silver moonlight to
The music of the gongs:
I've seen the luscious Dotty bring
Her errant lover back,
But Grables are unheard of on
The Island of Biak.

Behold the dusky siren with
Flat feet and kinky hair,

The men attired in G-strings soiled
The kids with bottoms bare;
Their mouths are stained with betel nut,
Bright red against the black -
'Tis these that we must live with on
The Island of Biak.

When the hellish day has ended and
The night birds drive us nuts,
When gnats and bugs and roaches play
At tag across our butts,
Composed at last for slumber on
The hard and dusty sack,
O how our inmost being damns
The Island of Biak.

Late in the month of July, we received our first pay since leaving Australia in mid-March. Because we were always paid in the local currency, we received our pay in Dutch East Indies bills. The basic unit was the gulden, or guilder, which, we were told, was worth fifty-three cents in U.S. currency. The money due each of us was calculated and paid to us in guilders. Because I had no need for money, I took almost all my pay for the five months to battalion headquarters and bought a money order at the rate of fifty-three cents U.S. currency per guilder and sent the money home.

About two weeks later, it was announced that the conversion rate at which we had been paid was incorrect; the guilder was really worth only forty cents. Consequently, a second pay call was issued and we received additional pay in guilders. I knew that I had received the pay due me because I had converted my guilders at the original rate, but I happily accepted the additional guilders. I immediately bought another money order and sent the money home. I looked upon my good fortune as a bonus from Uncle Sam.

We were not called upon to carry out many training exercises during that time, but we did pull shifts working on the beach as stevedores. At times the physical labor was difficult. I particularly remember transferring 200-lb. bombs from landing craft to trucks. The bombs were packed in wooden crates, which had to be picked up by two men and swung onto the truck bed about three and a half feet above the ground. One man would lift the nose end of the bomb, the other man the fin end. We would alternate ends because the weight was uneven, the nose end being much heavier. It was a difficult and very tiring job for me, particularly when the nose of the bomb was on my end of the crate.

Often we worked on the night shift. One night we were loading 55-gallon drums of aviation fuel onto trucks that would take them to the Mokmer airdrome. We were rolling the drums up planks on to the trucks when an air-raid alert was sounded. All lights were turned off and we stopped our work. I actually welcomed the alert because I was not feeling very well. I took advantage of the time off by lying on the beach next to the drums of explosive fuel. I don't recall if any planes came over that night.

A few nights later, we hit the jackpot. Our job for the night was to unload several boatloads of food. The food was assigned to an air force kitchen stationed on the island. I suppose the members of every outfit thought that their food was the worst, but when we saw what was being sent to the air force kitchen we could not believe our eyes. Fresh meat, fresh eggs, milk, and cookies were among the many treats being unloaded. We immediately decided that it was only fair that we should share in the bounty. After all, we were the ones who fought for two months to take the island from the Nips, so a "moonlight requisition" was in order. It was not difficult to find a truck driver who could be bribed. For the promise of a Japanese flag or bayonet, a side of beef or several cases of eggs could "fall" off the truck along the way. There were no bills of lading, so the contraband would never be missed.

In addition to making arrangements for the "deliveries," each of us sampled other items as we worked. There was the usual alert that night. Washing-Machine Charlie could be expected shortly after the moon had risen on most reasonably clear nights. I gained a little knowledge of astronomy because of Washing-Machine Charlie; I learned that the moon did not rise at the same time every night. During the alert, I "requisitioned" a huge can of pineapple slices, opened it with my little folding can opener, and enjoyed my treat while sitting on the beach. That night, during the blackout, we got our first look at the new P-61 Black Widow night-fighter as it climbed into the night sky to search for Charlie. The new twin-fuselage plane was aptly named; the entire plane was painted coal black.

As the month of August progressed, I began to feel weak and

very tired. By the middle of the month, I felt bad enough to go on sick call. I went to the battalion aid station where "Doc" Drexler, our battalion surgeon, looked at my eyes, took my temperature, and told me to go find a clear bottle somewhere and bring him a urine specimen. I searched the area around the aid station, found a bottle, and deposited the specimen. I was surprised to see that my urine was a dark reddish color. I presented the bottle to the doctor. He took one look at it and told me that I had hepatitis and jaundice. He said that he would sign me into a hospital for treatment.

After taking my gear to the supply tent, I went by boat on a short ride to Owi Island. A field hospital had been set up and an airstrip constructed by our Engineering Corps was in operation there. After only one day at Owi, I was informed that I would be going to a hospital at Hollandia. I was about to take my first plane trip.

That afternoon when a group of fellow patients and I reached the airstrip, we were greeted with a smile by the first white woman I had seen in almost five months, an army nurse. She was dressed in a flight suit, but she looked great. The sight of a pretty girl, combined with the fact that I was leaving Biak, gave my morale an immediate boost. I was happy as I boarded the plane, a C-47 transport.

The interior of the plane was furnished with two long wooden benches that ran parallel to the length of the body of the plane. Passengers sat facing each other. There was room in the aisle for a few men who were on stretchers. We usually referred to C-47s as "Biscuit Bombers" because they were often used to drop rations by parachute. The twin-engine, slow-moving transports were not armed and usually flew without armed escorts. Because the cabin was not pressurized, the plane flew over the ocean at a relatively low altitude. My first plane ride was noisy, but smooth and uneventful.

The hospital at Hollandia was much larger than the one on Owi. It was made up of large tents, each holding about twenty cots furnished with sheets, soft pillows, and, of course, mosquito netting. I was assigned a bed and instructed to stay in it except for visits to the latrine and the mess hall. I was more than happy to obey.

The next morning, an orderly wearing a white shirt and trousers came into our tent. He was carrying a white wooden case filled with glass vials. Printed in red on the outer side of the carrying case were the words "Doctor Dracula." He took blood samples from many of us and left. The next morning, we were once again greeted by "Doctor Dracula," who announced that he needed to take another set of blood samples. When pressed for a reason he reluctantly admitted that there had been a snafu in identifying the samples taken the previous day. This announcement drew remarks from some of my fellow patients that are best not repeated here.

My time in the hospital was spent reading, lounging, sleeping, and eating. I can't remember taking any medication other than Atabrine. The food was great compared to our normal fare. We had fresh meat, butter, and even a fresh egg one morning. It was really a treat. After a few days, I started to feel stronger and more lively. We had movies most nights, and I was allowed to attend. There were no air raids or even alerts to interrupt the shows. One night there was a live show featuring Bob Hope, Frances Langford, Jerry Colonna, and Tony Romano. Bob Hope's routine was greeted with cheers and laughter, but Frances Langford, clad in a slinky evening gown, received the loudest and most enthusiastic applause.

During my stay at the hospital, some of the patients in our tent were being treated for malaria. The treatment at that time was medication with Atabrine, bed rest, and drinking large quantities of water. For those who were seeking a way out of the army, malaria that would not respond to treatment was a favorite avenue of escape. The strategy employed to prolong the disease was obvious: omit the medication and avoid the intake of large amounts of water. The army, of course, recognized the ploy and devised ways to assure that the prescribed treatment was carried out.

The first two parts of the treatment were easily controlled: Atabrine was taken in the presence of a nurse or orderly, and bed rest could be easily monitored. Ensuring that the proper amount of water was ingested was a little more difficult, but a system had been devised to check compliance. A form with columns headed "intake" and "output" was attached to the foot of each bed. The patient recorded each glass of water consumed in the intake column, and once each day the nurse recorded the volume of the urine, which had been saved by the patient, in the output column. If the columns did not show the proper relationship, foul play was exposed.

The average GI was very resourceful, however. One man in our tent had devised a plan to beat the system. He easily falsified the intake column by recording more than his actual intake of water. To ensure that he could supply enough output to match the intake figures was more difficult. His urine could not be watered down; that was too easily detectable. But if he could add real urine to his bottle, he had found a way to falsify the records. The scheming GI went from bed to bed asking for donations. Most of us turned him down. We figured that if we were to spend the rest of the war in the Pacific, so should he. I don't know if his plan was eventually successful or not; he was still in the hospital when I was released to rejoin Company I.

After two weeks of rest and nourishing food, I began to feel much better, and I expected to be sent back to my outfit. I was in no hurry to give up the easy life that I was enjoying as a hospital patient, so I requested a dental checkup. A visit to the dentist, whose chair was set up outdoors in a tent, revealed two cavities. The next morning the dentist, using a drill powered by an assistant pumping a foot pedal, removed the decay and filled my teeth. I doubt that the drill could be described as high-speed, but it did the job.

Before I was discharged from the hospital, I was weighed and found that I had lost twenty pounds since leaving San Francisco. I weighed in at an even 130 pounds. A few days later, I was released from the hospital, boarded a ship, and began my second journey to Biak. The landing this time was much less eventful than the first.

It was the first week in September when I rejoined my outfit. I had not received any mail while I was in the hospital, so I was looking forward to having a big stack of letters when I rejoined Company I. Much to my disappointment, our mail clerk, George Wellwerts, told me that he had recently sent my mail to the hospital in Hollandia. I would have to wait for it to make the round trip. A few days later, I received about forty letters and several packages. Among the items in the packages was a small Kodak Brownie camera in an imitation-leather carrying case. I found the snap so badly rusted that when I tried to pull it open, it tore out of the case. When I tried to load the camera, I discovered that the film layer had softened and was sticking to the backing of the film layer beneath it. The heat, humidity, and salt air played havoc with many things. Envelopes and stamps stuck together, most articles made of iron rusted, and mildew grew on paper, cloth, and leather. On the equator it was hot, steamy summer throughout the entire year.

I often wrote home to request socks, T-shirts, and razor blades, items that were always in short supply. For some reason, the army seemed to be unable to supply us with enough socks or undershirts. I had just thrown away my last pair of socks and was doing without when a package containing socks arrived from home. I liked wearing a short-sleeved T-shirt rather than my heavy long-sleeved fatigue shirt while working around camp. The sun was too hot to go without a shirt; also, there was a rule, usually not enforced, against working or playing stripped to the waist.

As the days passed, our fortunes continued to improve. The food gradually became more varied. Fresh meat was occasionally added to our normal menu of corned "bully" beef, Spam, Vienna sausages, canned vegetables, dehydrated potatoes, and powdered eggs. At times we received a beer ration, usually about five or six cans for each man. We had no refrigeration, of course, but most of us enjoyed the warm beer anyway. We opened the cans very carefully by using the tip of a bayonet to pierce a tiny hole in the top. The trick was to get one's mouth quickly over the hole to consume the geyser of hot beer that erupted. After the pressure was relieved, we would then enlarge the hole with a bayonet and leisurely drink the rest of the beer.

As we made our way through the chow line one morning, we heard the unexpected but welcome news that we would have ice cream for dessert that night. Because ice cream was one of my favorite treats, I happily looked forward to the evening meal. As I reached the end of the chow line that evening, I received a big scoop of chocolate ice cream in one of the compartments in my mess kit. Imagine my disappointment when I tasted my first spoonful and found that it was so sour I could not swallow it. My first ice cream since leaving Australia and I could not eat it! Two weeks later, the sequence of events was repeated, this time with a happy ending. The ice cream was delicious.

The atmosphere at our camp during that time was relaxed and informal. Our officers slept and ate apart from the enlisted men, but that was about the only recognition of rank that I remember. We were not required to salute the officers, and the noncoms did not wear stripes. We called most of the noncoms by their first names. However, there was no lack of discipline. For the most part, though, the noncoms, who were all members of the division when it went overseas, associated with other noncoms, and the privates, most of whom were replacements, hung out with each other. Regardless of rank, the trials and hardships of combat had created feelings of comradeship and mutual respect among members of the company who had endured and survived those difficult, tiring, and sometimes terrifying days and nights of combat together. Despite some disagreements, we were a relatively happy family.

Most of the problems that did surface were associated with alcohol. There was one man in the company, a tall, lanky, young southerner who usually got along with everyone. He was quiet, easygoing, pleasant, and very slow-moving; we called him Speedball. However, when he drank, Speedball was transformed into a loud, trouble-seeking, obnoxious individual. Almost without fail he would get into a fight that would end with him battered and bruised. He was not much of a fighter. The next morning would find a repentant Speedball, usually with black eyes and split lips, apologizing and seeking forgiveness.

In our off hours, playing cards was one of the favorite ways to pass time. Many of the guys played poker, some losing several months' pay in one night, others winning large amounts. Payday overseas did not occur regularly. It was not unusual for us to go two or three months without pay. The evening of payday signaled the beginning of an all-night poker game. I was smart enough to know that those games were out of my league. Besides, I was sending virtually all my paychecks home. There was nothing to do with money but buy booze or gamble it away. In the jungles of New Guinea there were no prostitutes, there was no place to go, and there was nothing but liquor to buy. Two problems affecting most armies, venereal disease and AWOL, were almost nonexistent. Unless one could somehow get aboard a plane or a ship, there was no way out.

Like many of the other men, I spent a lot of time playing cards. My two buddies from New York, Arthur Smith and Sal Ferrara, usually played against Stacy Wilson and me. We played either casino or pinochle. No money was involved—only bragging rights. We had become close friends during the campaign and enjoyed being together and razzing each other. We spent many evenings playing cards by candlelight while sitting on our bunks.

When I think about the men with whom I spent almost two years of my life, one man, Kenneth Greene, is surely the most unforgettable. Ken, a fairly tall, very thin man in his mid-twenties, was from La Moure, North Dakota. I first noticed him aboard ship during the trip from Australia to New Guinea. Ken carried a bingo set in his barracks bag, and he spent many hours calling out numbers while running a bingo game. He collected the money, paid half of the pot to the winner, and kept the other half for himself. Obviously, he was an entrepreneur operating his one-man enterprise.

However, he was more than a businessman; he was a very good soldier. I can still picture Ken as a first scout advancing along a jungle trail. His appearance was certainly not that of a veteran jungle fighter, which indeed he was. Ken was very fair skinned and wore thick glasses. He never seemed to get a suntan; his face, and particularly his nose, were usually red and peeling. Instead of a steel helmet, Ken wore a Frank Buck–type straw hat that was painted an olive drab color. To complete his uniform, he wore a blue bandanna as a sweatband over his forehead. Rather than a tommy gun, which most first scouts carried, Ken preferred an M1 rifle with fixed bayonet.

Ken's actions in combat belied his appearance. He seemed to be as fearless and aggressive as they came. I was told that he had turned down promotions because he preferred to continue to serve as first scout. I don't know if that was true, but I do know that being a first scout offered good opportunities to pursue another of his businesses, collecting Japanese souvenirs. He would take any item of value if he thought he could carry it. I marveled at the size of his huge pack. I could not believe what he would do to acquire some of the souvenirs that he sold after the fighting ended. He seemed to think nothing of searching the pockets of dead Japanese soldiers, whose bodies were sometimes in advanced stages of decay. Among the items that Ken carried were a small rubber bag and a pair of pliers. The pliers were used to extract gold teeth from the fallen enemy. The rubber bag, of course, was used for storage of the booty. Because many of the Japanese had gold teeth, Ken's rubber bag filled rather quickly. Although several other men in the company collected gold teeth, most of us had no interest in such a gruesome activity.

After the fighting on Biak ended and we had set up camp,

another of Ken's enterprises came to my attention. Somewhere in the jungle reasonably close to our camp he set up and began operating a still. He had acquired a copper coil—in Australia, I presume. The other essentials, including ingredients, pots, and bottles were probably obtained by working with the mess sergeant. I really have only presumptions about how he pulled it off, but he was in production, making jungle juice, or white lightning, which he sold for the equivalent of twenty dollars a bottle, a lot of money in those days. Ken was sending so much money home that he was questioned by a battalion officer about the source of the money. Apparently the officer found it hard to believe that Ken could consistently win that much money playing poker. Never one to be without a solution to a problem, Ken sought out other members of the company who, for a small commission, sent money home for him.

There was only one occasion when I had business dealings with Ken. He would usually sell the Japanese souvenirs at the airstrip. Pilots always seemed to have money and were his best customers. I had picked up a Japanese flag that was partially burned. I didn't think it was worth sending home, so I talked to Ken and he said that he would try to sell it for me. We agreed to split anything he could get on a fifty-fifty basis. A few days later, he came to my tent and handed me a wad of guilders. I don't remember the amount, but it was much more than I had expected. When I asked him how he had gotten so much for a damaged flag, he just smiled. I pressed him for an answer. He said that he had offered two other flags to a pilot, but the man balked at the price Ken wanted. Ken then told him that he had another flag (mine) that he could sell at a slightly lower price. When the pilot saw the burned flag, he was not interested; but Ken, like any good salesman, did not give up easily. He told the man that there was a story to go with that particular flag. He then went on to relate how we had surrounded a pillbox but the Nips would not surrender, so the pillbox was sprayed with a flame thrower. The Japs came running out, their clothing on fire, one carrying the burning flag. The story was a hoax, but the pilot bought it. He said he preferred that flag because it came with a story that he could tell his friends.

During the summer of 1944, something very much out of the ordinary was happening back home in St. Louis: the St. Louis Browns were in first place in the American League pennant race. Even though the Cardinals were the more successful and popular team in St. Louis, the Browns were my favorite. As the season progressed and the Browns continued to lead the league, I enjoyed razzing my two New York buddies. However, during the last two weeks of the season, both the New York Yankees and the Detroit Tigers moved ahead of the Browns. I took a lot of abuse from the New Yorkers, but on the last day of the season, the Washington Senators beat the Tigers, while the Browns trounced the Yankees to win their first American League pennant. To make things even better, the Cardinals were winners of the National League flag. I received the happy news from Bernie Schimmel, our supply sergeant. Bernie and I had become friends, and he knew that I was a big Browns fan. Smitty and Sal declared that if the Browns could win the pennant, they expected the war to end any day. The story did not have a perfect ending, though; the Cards won the World Series in six games.

Because Biak was located about sixty miles south of the equator, it was a land of perpetual summer. Daytime temperatures often exceeded 100°F, rainstorms were frequent, and the air was extremely humid. Nevertheless, those conditions did not keep us from enjoying a few sporting events of our own. We constructed a softball field by building a backstop and leveling the coral surface with a bulldozer. This created an almost snow-white but relatively smooth surface. We formed a team and played games against other outfits. I played left field. We also had a volleyball team that played matches against other companies. These matches were usually played in the early evening and drew good crowds. The Company I team was very good and more than held its own against the other outfits. I did not play on the team, but I enjoyed watching the games and cheering for our team. George Ludwig, Bernie Schimmel, Paul Price, and Charles Spangler were the players I remember.

A bit of good news was announced by a general order dated August 19, 1944: I, along with 133 other members of Company I, had been awarded the Combat Infantryman Badge as a result of "having conducted ourselves in an exemplary manner in action against the enemy." I was proud and happy to receive the award. I still look upon it as one of my most valued possessions. I'm certain that only those who fought as infantrymen can understand what the award means to those who have earned it. In addition to its sentimental value, the badge had a monetary value: a $10-per-month raise. I was getting into the big money. My gross pay increased to $74.80 per month. The other good news concerned the progress of the war both in Europe and in the Pacific. The success of our offensives in both theaters was very encouraging.

Early in the month of October, I learned that I had been chosen to attend some classes at what was described as Intelligence School. I was happy for a break in our routine, which had become rather boring. When I reported to the classroom tent a few days later, about a dozen students were assembled there. Apparently it had been decided that it would be desirable for someone in each company to learn semaphore so that signals could be sent to ships offshore if radios were not available. I suspect that the accidental shelling we suffered by one of our destroyers that third day of the campaign might have spawned that idea. Whatever the reason, we were handed flags and began learning the signals for the letters of the alphabet. I can still remember the signals for A through K, but nothing more. We also learned a few words of Japanese. We were instructed in the reading of topographical maps and learned a little about reading aerial photos by measuring shadows to determine the heights of structures. The schooling lasted for a week, and we were then given a test on the subject matter.

After the tests were graded, an officer told me that I had done very well and asked me if I would be interested in a transfer into Intelligence. Such a thought had never crossed my mind, but after a few seconds I could picture myself sitting at a glass-topped desk in Hawaii interpreting aerial photos or breaking Japanese code messages. Was this finally that "good spot" I had been promised on my first day in the army? I told the officer that I might be interested and asked for more information. He went on to explain that there were some openings in the I&R (Intelligence and Reconnaissance) platoon. A different picture flashed across my mental screen. I saw myself leading a patrol behind enemy lines or paddling a rubber raft toward a beach weeks before an upcoming landing to gather information concerning enemy positions and strengths. I immediately decided to stay with my outfit. I informed the officer of my decision, was dismissed, and went back to join Company I.

Throughout the campaigns for Papua and the rest of New

Guinea, MacArthur had only one U.S. Army under his command, the Sixth Army, commanded by General Krueger. In anticipation of the upcoming Philippine invasion, another army had been created, and General Eichelberger was named commander. The 41st Division had been a part of the Sixth Army; but with the formation of the Eighth Army, our division became a member of that new army.

It was mid-October when we learned about the landings on Leyte in the Philippines. By this time, some of the men who had not been seriously wounded had returned. A few of the original members of the company who had been granted furloughs were returning. Replacements were arriving to fill the spots of those who would not return. The company was nearing full strength, and we knew that it was only a matter of time until we would be in action again.

Most of the new men seemed very young to me. My thoughts returned to the time, nine months earlier, when I joined the company. I'm sure that I looked very young to the veterans at that time. Even to an outsider, it would have been a simple task to pick out a newcomer, just by looking at the normal color of his skin as compared to the yellow, Atabrine-stained, sun-baked skin of the veterans. The continual use of the yellow Atabrine pills caused the skin to take on an obvious yellow cast that was only partially hidden by a suntan. The color was particularly noticeable on parts of the body that were not exposed to the sun. My feet were a very bright yellow. The coloring matter in the Atabrine was so strong that one man dissolved some pills in water and used the solution to dye a white T-shirt a vivid canary yellow.

Thanksgiving arrived, and we had no news of an impending move. In a letter to my sister, I related the events of the holiday: "Yesterday was Thanksgiving. We had a parade in the morning after which I attended Mass. For dinner we had the best food that I had tasted since leaving the U.S. We had fresh eggs, tomatoes, and cucumbers, followed by roast turkey, cranberry sauce, hot rolls, pumpkin pie and oranges. Of course it wasn't as good as Mom's cooking, but I really enjoyed the meal."

Shortly after Thanksgiving, George Cooley informed me that I would take over as the bazooka man for the platoon. The man who previously carried the bazooka had been wounded and would not return to the company. I was not happy with the new assignment.

The bazooka, or rocket launcher, anti-tank MI, fired a rocket 2.36 inches in diameter capable of penetrating three inches of armor. The weapon with the rocket weighed eighteen pounds and was about five feet long. It was a difficult job to carry it through the jungle. Because of its length, it often became entangled in vines or low tree branches. It was a tough job even for a big man; it would have been extremely hard for me. I have never considered myself a salesman, but I was successful, after considerable pleading, in convincing George that I would not be a good bazooka man.

The next day Sergeant Cooley told me that I would have a different assignment. My new job would be to serve as runner for our new platoon leader, Lieutenant Armstrong. My duties as runner in combat would be to accompany the lieutenant wherever he went and deliver any messages he wished to send to anyone in the company. The bad part of the job was that there might be extra exposure to fire while moving about to deliver messages, but the good part was that I would sleep in the interior of the perimeter near the lieutenant. No more guard shifts three times every night! I was more than happy with my new assignment.

December 8th arrived, marking the third anniversary of Pearl Harbor (the date of the attack was December 8th on the west side of the international date line). Christmas packages began to arrive as we continued to prepare for the next move. We received necessary supplies and any needed inoculations. One of the new items issued to us was a new type of boot that made leggings obsolete. The new boots were called combat boots. The upper portion of the combat boots came to almost mid-calf and could be unbuckled to allow the bottom part of the trousers to be tucked in, thus eliminating the need for leggings. I traded in my old size 9B boots for a new pair of size 10A combat boots.

I am certain that we carried out some training exercises during that period, but I can recall only a few of them. I do remember firing my M1 on the 1,000-inch range. On that miniature range, we fired our rifles at a mini-target from a distance of 1,000 inches, approximately 83 feet. The bull's-eye, as best I can remember, was about the size of a half-dollar. The entire target was about 12 to 15 inches in diameter.

One afternoon we were ordered to fall out and line up to practice close-order drill. It had been more than a year since I participated in such a training exercise, and I was not enthusiastic about the prospect of drilling on the rough coral under the blistering New Guinea sun. My feelings were shared by most of the men. We protested, but to no avail. With a sergeant calling the commands, the drill began. It was a disaster. We looked like a group of raw recruits. After a short but futile effort the sergeant gave up. It was difficult, if not impossible, to convince a group of combat veterans that we would learn anything that would benefit us in our next campaign by practicing close-order drill on a sweltering afternoon.

Late in the year we were introduced to two new weapons. One was a bazooka that could be broken down into three sections, each about two feet long. This was an improvement, because it was much easier to carry through the jungle than the original one-piece bazooka. However, our introduction to the new bazooka was the occasion of an unfortunate accident.

The company was assembled in a clearing near our camp, a target was chosen, and the demonstration of the new weapon began. The bazooka gunner and his assistant were in prone positions facing the target, and the remainder of the company took up positions to watch the firing of the weapon. No one could be directly behind the bazooka because of the rear blast when the weapon was fired, so most of us lined up to either side of and somewhat behind the bazooka crew. However, a number of men lined up to the side but ahead of the gunner, leaving him a corridor of ten or fifteen yards to fire through at the target, which was a safe distance from everyone. When all was in readiness the gunner squeezed the trigger, but the bazooka did not fire. However, as the gunner began to rise, he released the trigger and the weapon fired. At that moment, the muzzle of the weapon was angled slightly toward the ground, and the rocket hit the ground and exploded twenty or thirty yards from the gunner, but within a short distance of some of the men lined up ahead of the weapon. Several men were wounded, I don't know how seriously. It was an accident that could have been avoided. No one should have been closer to the target than the man firing the bazooka.

The other new weapon was a small hand-held .45-caliber machine gun. We called the new weapon "grease gun" because it looked a lot like a grease gun. It was only about sixteen or eighteen inches long, and its stock was constructed of stamped metal parts. We evaluated the weapon by firing it at a 55-gallon oil drum. When the bullets just bounced off the drum, most of us quickly lost interest in the weapon. I don't think anyone in our company ever carried a grease gun. It was a poor substitute for a tommy gun.

During the week before Christmas, I attended a mission and had the opportunity to serve Mass. On Christmas Eve, I attended midnight Mass. We had a good meal on Christmas Day and another on New Year's Day. Everyone was happy that we had been able to spend the Christmas season free of combat. In early January, we learned about the Luzon landings. Finally, the expected announcement was made. We would break camp later in the week. On January 20th, we boarded a troop transport. Everyone expected that our destination would be Luzon.

The ship and particularly the meals were pleasant surprises. We had fresh meat, fresh bread and butter, Jell-O, soda, and even ice cream. I met several sailors from St. Louis. One was a lieutenant who had attended St. Louis University High School with several fellows that I knew. We heard news that the Russians were within 100 miles of Berlin and that our forces on Luzon were within thirty miles of Manila. It seemed that Manila might fall before we reached Luzon.

When we arrived at our destination, we were in the Philippines, but the island on which we debarked was not Luzon; it was Mindoro, which had been taken about six weeks earlier by the 24th Division. We learned that we had been in the reserve for the Luzon campaign, but General MacArthur decided that the 41st Division would not be needed on Luzon; instead, the division would take the lead in the liberation of the Southern Philippines.

As soon as we stepped ashore on Mindoro Island, we saw huge differences between New Guinea and this Philippine island. The Filipino people, of course, were obviously different in appearance. Many of them could speak at least some English, and some spoke English very well. Some of the young women were very pretty. They were all very friendly and greeted us warmly. They expressed a hatred toward the Japanese and related many stories about the ill-treatment they had suffered under the Japanese rule.

The Filipino women were happy to wash our clothes for a small fee, and almost all the GIs took advantage of the service that was offered. We would often see women walking along the roads carry-ing huge bundles of laundry on their heads. They would take the clothing to the nearest stream, where they washed it by beating the clothes with large wooden paddles.

There was also a major difference in the climate from that of New Guinea. Although the days were still hot, the nights were definitely cooler, and the humidity was not nearly so high. The rain-fall, at least at that time of the year, was considerably less. In fact, the roads were actually quite dusty. There were a few old cars and trucks on the roads. There were also narrow-gauge railroad tracks, but I don't recall ever seeing a train. We saw cattle, pigs, chickens, and other domestic animals. We learned that cock-fighting was a fa-vorite sport of the Filipinos and, of course, it only took a day or two until a few GIs had bought roosters and were holding cockfights of their own. That new sport did not last very long, because the roost-ers started crowing very early in the morning; before long most of them ended up as meals for their owners. I never tasted any of the roosters, but I did have fresh fish one evening. One of my buddies, Cliff Cole, and I took a few hand grenades and went fishing in a nearby stream. We came back after a short time with six or eight nice fish. Those hand grenades worked much better and faster than any fishing pole I have ever used.

The camp that we set up on Mindoro was near the town of San Jose. I made a trip into town one Sunday afternoon, and I remem-ber seeing cockfights, but I don't recall much else about the town.

Before we started to set up camp on Mindoro, the supply ser-geant, Bernie Schimmel, offered me a job working in the supply tent; I quickly accepted. I had become friendly with Bernie, who was one of the veteran members of the company. He had been a minor-league baseball player and was a big fan of the Detroit Tigers, his home team. I knew that I would enjoy working with Bernie and Jack Wil-liams, who was the company armorer. Another thing I liked was that I would not have to pull KP duty or any other details as long as I worked in the supply room.

We had been on Mindoro only three weeks when we learned that the 186th Infantry had invaded Palawan, an island in the southwestern Philippines. The 41st Division was in combat again. The Palawan landing took place on February 28th. A few days later, we learned that the rest of the division would make an assault landing on March 10, 1945 at Zamboanga, a city on the extreme southwesterly tip of Mindanao, the second largest island in the Philippines. The code name given to the operation was VICTOR IV. The plan for the landing called for the 162nd Infantry to make up the assault waves, landing about four miles northwest of the city of Zamboanga. Our first objective would be Wolfe airstrip, about a half mile inland. The 163rd Infantry would follow us ashore and move to the southeast to capture San Roque airstrip and then the city of Zamboanga.

6

Zamboanga
VICTOR IV

On March 8th, our battalion boarded an LST that was to become
part of a 200-ship convoy under the command of Admiral Forest
Royal.[1] The LST, a large, shallow-draft, ocean-going ship that was
328 feet long and 50 feet wide, was capable of carrying troops and
supplies plus trucks, tanks, and small landing craft. Because of its
large size and because it usually traveled at a speed of only eight
or nine knots, it was sometimes called "large slow target" rather
than "landing ship tank." We were aboard an LST because we
were to make the landing in LVTs, which were carried on the tank
deck of the ship. Although our entire battalion was aboard the
LST, there were bunks for only 160 men plus the ship's crew, so
most of us had to find a place to sleep. The top deck was covered
with military vehicles of every imaginable type, but Stacy and I
were able to find a spot under a big truck, where we bunked during
the journey to Zamboanga.

While we were en route I found a spare life preserver, cut it open,
and removed some of the kapok that filled it. I filled a small rubber
bag with the kapok and used it as a foxhole pillow throughout the remainder of the war. I found it to be a big improvement over the air-
filled pillow I had been using.

1. Morison, *The Liberation of the Philippines*, p. 222.

After an uneventful voyage, we arrived at our destination early on the morning of March 10, 1945. At about 0815 we went below to the tank deck of the LST, where we climbed aboard the landing craft. The LVTs, or buffaloes, were tracked amphibious vehicles with an overall length of only twenty-six feet. Each LVT could carry about twenty men. I had been aboard an LVT twice at Biak, the first time when we made our withdrawal from Mokmer Village, the second when we bypassed the Parai Defile and landed at Parai Village. Both of these operations started and ended on land. We were now about to set out on a water-to-land operation that would begin quite differently. The LST had two large vertical doors at the bow of the ship. Those doors could be opened at sea and a ramp from the tank deck could then be lowered into the ocean. The LVTs would use the ramp to make their entry into the water.

That morning before the doors were opened, the coxswain of our landing craft warned us that when the buffalo went off the ramp into the water, the front of the vehicle would tip sharply forward and some water would come in. He told us to get as far aft as possible and hang on. He assured us that the water that we would take in would quickly drain out. He closed his short speech by saying, "There's nothing to worry about." He did not convince me; I worried anyway.

The use of life preservers was a matter that always seemed ironic to me. When we were aboard large ships such as a transport or an LST, we were required to have a life preserver with us at all times; but when we boarded small landing craft to make our assaults, life preservers were discarded. Of course, I understood the reasons; nevertheless, that morning when our buffalo was about to dive into the Sulu Sea, it would have been comforting to have been wearing a life preserver rather than a heavy pack.

As the doors of the LST swung open, the motors of the landing craft were started and, in spite of the circulation system, the air filled with exhaust fumes from the diesel engines. The ramp was lowered and the buffaloes began to make their way down the ramp and dive into the water. Our turn came. The LVT slowly climbed a slight incline to reach the doorway and started down the ramp. The vehicle made its descent with its treads clanking against the steel ribs of the ramp. As it reached the end of the ramp, it tipped forward at a sharp angle and plunged into the sea. Water rushed in and I was sure we were going down, but the craft quickly leveled, the water drained out, and I drew a sigh of relief as we bobbed on the waves.

The coxswains then maneuvered the LVTs into circles. Each circle was composed of vehicles for a specific assault wave. While the waves continued to form, the naval and aerial bombardment of the beachhead area began. Two cruisers and six destroyers fired salvo after salvo on their targets. There was no answering fire from the shore. As the bombardment progressed, the buffaloes continued to circle offshore near the line of departure. As we circled, we breathed the exhaust fumes that were becoming very heavy, and I began to feel sick. To this day, the odor of exhaust gases from diesel engines reminds me of landing craft. H-hour was scheduled for 0915, and the landing was proceeding on schedule. B-24 Liberators of the Thirteenth Air Force dropped their bombs, and the time for our assault was at hand.[2] The circles of LVTs were transformed into lines parallel to the beach, and the attack waves started toward the shore; our LVT was in the first wave.

As we slowly made our way toward the landing beach about four and a half miles northwest of Zamboanga City, the shelling seemed to be reaching a crescendo. The sound and intensity of the bombardment gave me a feeling of excitement and confidence. An LCIR, an LCI converted into a rocket ship, was immediately to the right of our landing craft as we approached the beach. The ship was firing salvos of 4.5-inch rockets as it escorted us to the shore. The barrage continued until our first wave of landing craft climbed onto the beach. We jumped out of the buffaloes and moved quickly across an open field toward the Wolfe airstrip half a mile ahead as General Eichelberger watched from the deck of the destroyer *Rocky Mount*. There was a little machine-gun fire coming from our left flank, but it was soon silenced. We had landed against very light opposition, which was fortunate because we had no cover whatsoever as we moved toward the airdrome.

As we moved inland, Japanese artillery and mortar fire began to hit the beachhead area behind us. The Japs had begun to fight back. My job now was to stick close to our platoon leader, Lieutenant Armstrong, a big man who wore a large bushy mustache. He

2. Morison, *The Liberation of the Philippines*, pp. 222, 224.

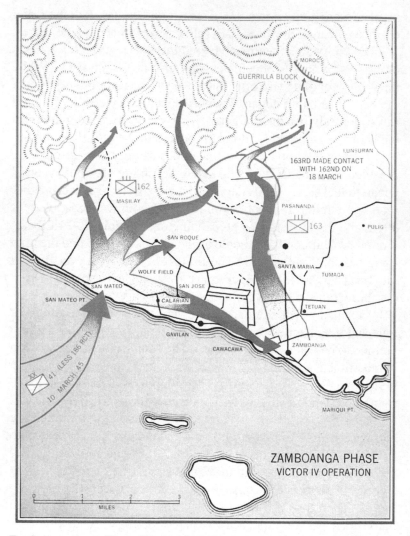

Zamboanga phase, Victor IV operation. From McCartney, *The Jungleers.*

was older than most of the men, probably in his late thirties. I had an extra piece of equipment to carry this time, a walkie-talkie radio. To compensate somewhat for the additional weight of the radio, I had decided not to carry a bayonet. I reasoned that the only time I would need a bayonet would be if I were out of ammunition. I thought that the chance of that happening was rather slim, so I pitched my bayonet overboard the night before the landing. I chose to keep my M1 rather than to carry a carbine, which was about half the weight of an M1. The M1 had better accuracy, a longer range, and higher muzzle velocity than the carbine. I felt that it was well worth carrying the extra four pounds of weight to keep those advantages. Also, I had lived for almost two years with an M1 in my hands or at my side, and I had acquired a feeling of great confidence in the weapon.

The Japanese artillery fire continued, and two LSTs were hit. Continuing our advance, we reached the Wolfe airstrip and moved on toward the village of San Roque. The Japs had constructed an elaborate system of pillboxes and trenches, but they had abandoned them during the pre-landing bombardment and had not been able to re-enter them because of our swift advance. We met no serious opposition during the first day, and on the first night we set up our perimeter in one of those abandoned fortifications.

By the end of the second day, the 163rd Infantry, which followed us ashore, had captured the city of Zamboanga and the San Roque airstrip against light resistance and the 162nd Infantry had taken control of the coastal plain north of the city. The Japanese had retreated to prepared defensive positions in the high ground overlooking the airstrips and the city.

Intelligence about the Zamboanga area came from a band of Filipino guerrillas commanded by Colonel Wendell Fertig, a U.S. Army reservist. The guerrillas had held out in the rain forests of Mindanao during the Japanese occupation.[3] A few days after our landing, we made contact with a group of the guerrillas. They were overjoyed to see us and told us how they had continued to harass the Japanese throughout the three years of their occupation. The guerrillas claimed that they had killed many Japs during that time. The men said that their officers ordered them to cut off the right ear of any Jap they had slain and present it as proof that they had killed one of the hated enemy.

Information from the guerrillas indicated that the main Japanese defensive positions were on the slopes of Mount Capisan, about two miles north of San Roque, and on Mount Pulungbata,

3. Smith, *Triumph in the Philippines,* p. 592.

about five miles inland. Approximately 9,000 enemy troops of the Independent Mixed Brigade under the command of Lieutenant General Tokichi Hojo held excellent defenses overlooking the entire tip of the Zamboanga peninsula.[4] The U.S. attack plan called for the 163rd Infantry to clear the Japanese from Mount Pulungbata while the 162nd attacked the enemy on Mount Capisan.

We had left behind the hot, steamy jungles of New Guinea, but now we faced the roadless, lush rain forest of southern Mindanao. The slopes of Mount Capisan were so steep and overgrown that tanks were useless. We relied on our mortars, on artillery, and on the planes of the Marine Aircraft Groups 12 and 32 for support. The planes were based at an airstrip at Dupolog, about 150 miles north of Zamboanga. The strip had been held by the Filipinos throughout the Japanese occupation.[5] Our advances were limited not only by the stubborn resistance of the Japs but also by the time required by the 116th Engineers to build a road behind us. Bulldozers followed immediately behind us as the "cats" scraped a crude road through the forest. The road was needed to bring supplies of ammunition, food, and water to us and to evacuate the dead and wounded GIs. I admired the ability and guts of the engineers as we watched them work within range of the enemy guns.

Although I was not enjoying our return to combat, I did very much appreciate the privilege of sleeping in the center of the perimeter. Instead of sleeping in a three-man hole, I shared my foxhole, which was always close to the hole of our platoon leader, with Martin Lee, the medic assigned to our platoon. Marty was a young man, possibly a year or two older than I. He was a quiet, conscientious GI from Brooklyn, New York. Marty suffered a minor shrapnel wound during the Zamboanga campaign, but he stayed with the company until the fighting came to an end.

The role of medics assigned to a line infantry company was not an enviable one. They were exposed to as much danger as we infantrymen, and sometimes more. They endured the same hardships that we did; in addition, they were under the stress of trying to treat the wounded and dying while being subjected to enemy fire. More

4. Smith, *Triumph in the Philippines*, pp. 593–595.
5. Sherrod, *History of Marine Corps Aviation in World War II*, p. 316.

often than not, more than one man needed help at the same time. I know that to me one of the most disheartening sounds of combat was the cry of "Medic!" that rang out when someone in our midst was wounded. I believe that the medics felt the same way.

Most of the medics had little or no medical background before their army service; they were trained after they were inducted into the army. They had little to work with in the field. Most treatments involved dusting the wound with sulfanilamide, trying to stop the flow of blood, bandaging the wound, and administering morphine and blood plasma, if needed. Evacuating the wounded was often a dangerous and difficult task. The casualty rate of the medics who were with our company seemed to be extraordinarily high. They suffered both battle and nonbattle casualties. The nonbattle casualties, mostly psychoneuroses, probably were caused by the pressures and conditions under which they carried out their duties. The contributions of the medics in the 41st Division were not overlooked; they received more decorations in proportion to their numbers than any other branch of the division.

As we made our slow advance up the slopes of Mount Capisan, there was one similarity to Biak that was most discouraging: we were under fire and were suffering casualties at the hands of Japs whom we almost never saw. A difference, though, was that as the Nips retreated they left behind areas that were often mined or booby-trapped. We learned that after driving the Japs from a hill, the 163rd Infantry suffered eighty-three casualties when the Japs detonated a buried ammunition dump and blew the top off the hill. After that incident, every patch of ground that we wrested from the Nips was hurriedly searched for any signs of buried explosives.

By the time we had advanced about halfway up the mountain, I had decided to lighten my load. I had carried the walkie-talkie radio since we landed and there had not been any occasion to use it. Also, I had never seen anyone successfully use that type of intercom at Hollandia or Biak. In the dense jungles, they never seemed to work satisfactorily. I decided that the next time we were under fire the radio would get lost. I did not have to wait long. The next day we were pinned down by fire from a Japanese Nambu light machine gun. Bullets were cutting leaves off the low-hanging branches just above my head. When the fire let up, we moved out and I "forgot" to bring the radio with me. It was not until several days later that Lieutenant Armstrong noticed that I was not carrying the walkie-talkie. When he asked me where the radio was I told him that I had left it on the ridge when we were under fire. Army, as he was known to the other officers, gave me a knowing look without saying a word. The subject never came up again. He was a good guy. I liked him.

My twenty-first birthday, which I "celebrated" near the top of Mount Capisan, was a birthday I remember very well. We spent most of the day crouching in our foxholes. The Japs fired machine guns and 20-mm anti-aircraft guns at us while our artillery fired shells over our heads, trying to silence the enemy fire. Someone volunteered the information that the Japs were violating the rules of war by using 20-mm explosive shells against personnel. That information, whether it was true or not, did little to comfort me; I knew that the Nips had little or no regard for those rules. I kept my head down until the Jap guns were silenced and we moved out again. Our casualties that day were one man killed and nine wounded.

The next morning as we looked down at the beach where we had landed a week earlier, we could not believe our eyes; another "assault landing" was taking place. Men in full battle dress were coming ashore by way of landing craft. A movie camera set up on the beach was photographing the event as staff members of a nearby field hospital watched. No one could offer an explanation of the proceedings, so we turned around and resumed our efforts to clear the Japs still clinging to the heights of Mount Capisan.

It was not until the next day when we saw the first Marine Corps planes land on San Roque airstrip that we figured out what had taken place the previous day. We had watched the ground crew members of the Marine Aircraft Groups arriving from the airstrip at Dupolog, where their planes had been based. Although we very much appreciated the excellent support provided for us by the Marine pilots and their ground crew members, we did not appreciate the theatrics of their "landing" on a beach we had secured a week earlier.

One of the good things that took place during the Zamboanga campaign was the substitution of new C-rations for the usual diet of K-rations. The new C-rations included cans of spaghetti and meatballs, chicken and rice, and frankfurters and beans. I know that my Italian father would have rebelled at the thought of canned spaghetti and meatballs, but everyone eagerly accepted any change from the daily routine of the hated K-rations.

After we had taken a high point near the top of the mountain one afternoon, we began to take fire from Japanese mortars. As I was about to hit the dirt, I saw a mortar shell land at the feet of one of our officers whose name I can't recall. He was probably about twenty feet from me and I watched as the force of the explosion threw him into the air. He landed on his back with blood streaming down his face. He was not killed, but he certainly appeared to be badly wounded. I had seen many men who were wounded, but I had never seen the actual explosion of a shell and its immediate effect on its victim. I will never forget that terrible sight.

A short time later that afternoon one of my best buddies, Sal Ferrara, was wounded. He suffered a shrapnel wound to his head. I vividly remember Sal being evacuated. He was able to walk, but his head was bandaged and blood was running down his face. As he passed me he said, "So long, Zero. Be careful." Sal was not seriously wounded; he rejoined the company about two months later.

That evening after Marty and I finished digging our hole, we put my poncho on the ground and set Marty's poncho aside for a cover, if needed. After our evening meal, we crawled into our hole and I quickly went to sleep. During the night, while I was sleeping on my back, I was jolted awake by what felt like a blow to my chest. My first thought was that a Jap had gotten into our hole and had hit me with the butt of his rifle. After an instant, however, when I realized that I was still alive and not even hurt, I began to think rationally. An animal—most probably a monkey—must have jumped out of a tree, landed on my chest, and quickly bounded out of the hole. After a few minutes to calm my shaken nerves, I was tired enough to go back to sleep.

By late March, we had eliminated the last organized resistance on Mount Capisan and enjoyed a spectacular view from the top of the mountain. The entire tip of the Zamboanga peninsula was visible from our viewpoint. The island of Basilan, a Moro stronghold, stood just offshore near the tip of the peninsula. Also visible were the city of Zamboanga—or what was left of it—and the San Roque airstrip, which was already in use. The foliage was lush and green;

the ocean was a deep blue. It was the most beautiful view I had seen since leaving San Francisco. While we held our position atop the mountain, the engineers completed the road to the top. At the point where the road ended they erected a wooden sign that read, "If you want to go higher, see the Chaplain." Signed: "116th Engineers."

A few days later, army trucks were sent up the mountain road to take us down to an area where we would set up camp. Our job at Zamboanga was finished. We climbed onto the trucks for a ride down the mountain. We had gone only a short distance before I was wishing that we had been allowed to walk. The road was muddy and slick. To make some of the hairpin turns on that primitive road, it was necessary for the driver to make a partial turn and back up before moving forward again. At many points there were sheer drop-offs within inches of the road. I prayed all the way down. By the time we were safely off that mountain, I had developed great admiration for the skill of the GIs who drove those trucks.

It had taken about three weeks to eliminate any organized Japanese resistance. During that time, about 6,400 Japanese were killed or died of disease or starvation. The combined casualties of our 162nd and 163rd Regiments were 220 men killed and 665 wounded.[6]

Shortly before we were relieved, elements of the 186th Infantry began to arrive from Palawan. Those troops pursued the Japanese who were trying to escape into the interior rain forest of Mindanao. The area surrounding Zamboanga was cleared by the end of April. During the fighting, the 186th Infantry killed 2,331 Japs and took 103 prisoners. The 186th Infantry losses were fifteen killed and thirty-nine wounded.[7]

Within a month of our landing on Zamboanga, four additional landings were carried out by elements of the 41st Division. Basilan Island, about ten miles south of Zamboanga, was taken by Company F of the 162nd Infantry without opposition on March 16th. The next landings were made by the 2nd Battalion of the 163rd Infantry. On April 2nd, those troops landed on Sanga Sanga, an island in the Tawi

6. Smith, *Triumph in the Philippines,* pp. 597–598.
7. Westerfield, *41st Infantry Division,* p. 224.

Tawi group of islands, about 200 miles southwest of Zamboanga and about forty miles from Borneo. The battalion also made a landing on nearby Bangao Island, where light opposition was encountered. Thirty Japanese were killed, and the U.S. losses were two men killed and four wounded. The final landing in the Sulu Archipelago was made by the remainder of the 163rd Infantry on Jolo Island, which was situated about midway between Basilan and the Tawi Tawi group of islands. The 163rd Infantry killed over 2,000 Japanese before being relieved in mid-June. The 163rd regiment losses were 35 men killed and 125 wounded.[8]

During a period of forty days, the 41st Division had regained from the Japanese the island of Palawan, the Zamboanga peninsula, and four islands of the Sulu Archipelago. After the successful completion of the landings, General MacArthur sent the following congratulatory message to General Doe:

> Palawan and Zamboanga represent splendid performances which reflect greatest credit on all concerned. Their perfect coordination and their complete success show the fighting services at their best. Please inform all ranks.[9]

When our battalion was relieved near the end of March, we set up camp in a beautiful coconut grove north of Zamboanga city. After a shower, a change to clean clothes, a hot meal, and a good night's sleep on a cot, my morale was much improved. The next day I received fifteen letters, two copies of the *St. Louis Post-Dispatch,* and a copy of the *Sporting News,* which my friend and future brother-in-law Vernon Thurmer sent to me throughout the war. I also received a package that had been mailed on November 21st, more than four months earlier. I was able to salvage a fruitcake, some figs, a can of deviled ham, and some socks. During the next few days, I enjoyed sights of civilization such as cornfields, vegetable gardens, banana groves, and domestic animals, including horses, water buffalo, and chickens. However, I did not enjoy the flies and mosquitoes; they were even worse than those in New Guinea.

Coconuts were plentiful, and we could get all that we wanted,

8. Smith, *Triumph in the Philippines,* pp. 597–598.
9. McCartney, *The Jungleers,* p. 154. Quote in McCartney.

but bananas were very hard to find. One afternoon I was approached by a Filipino man who offered to sell me a nice bunch of bananas. I don't remember the price he asked, but it was much lower than I expected. I quickly paid the man and happily headed for my tent with my "bargain" bunch of bananas. I noticed that the bananas were rather thick and short, but they were a nice yellow color; they looked fine to me. When I reached my tent I peeled and tasted one of them; it was very dry and mealy. I could not eat it. After some investigation I learned that I had purchased a bunch of cooking bananas. I had no way to cook the bananas, so I gave them to a young Filipino boy, who eagerly accepted them. For a small price, I learned a little bit about bananas that afternoon.

Soon after that, I was involved in another venture that did not turn out well. The Filipinos in the Zamboanga area brewed an alcoholic beverage called *tuba*. It was my understanding that the *tuba* was prepared by cutting the top off a coconut and then hanging the coconut, filled with its milk, in a tree until the milk fermented.

One afternoon several of us pitched in to buy a bottle of *tuba* from a local Filipino. The fermented milk was a cloudy dark orange color, and small pieces of coconut meat had settled to the bottom of the bottle. The appearance of the drink was not promising, but we went back to camp, got our canteen cups, and sampled our purchase. The taste was mild and rather sweet. It certainly tasted a lot better than it looked. A couple of other men joined us and we rather quickly emptied the bottle. It was only an hour or so until I started to feel sick to my stomach. I did not throw up but I had heartburn and a terrible sour taste in my mouth throughout the rest of the afternoon and evening. My only consolation was that I was not alone in my misery. I suffered throughout the night, but after eating some breakfast the next morning I began to feel better. I was never tempted to try that Filipino beverage again.

During the next few days, we heard news of several major events. The formation of another new army in the Pacific and the landing on Okinawa were encouraging developments. The news from Europe continued to be great. Obviously the war against Germany was about to end. We were all saddened by the unexpected news of President Roosevelt's sudden death. I wondered how well Harry Truman, a Missourian, would be able to handle the job of president of the United

States. About that time, word was received that all men over the age of forty were eligible for discharge. A small number of men in our company qualified and left for home. Another Easter came, and I was able to attend Mass and receive Holy Communion.

Shortly after Easter, I attended a show performed by a small group headed by Joe E. Brown. The cast included an accordion player, a violinist, and a juggler. I enjoyed the show, especially Joe's imitation of a baseball pitcher. It was the 648th overseas performance by Joe E. Brown during the war. I doubt that most people know how much he did to entertain U.S. servicemen and women.

7

Mindanao
VICTOR V

About four weeks after the end of the Zamboanga campaign, the 162nd Infantry was alerted for movement to the Parang-Cotabato region of Mindanao, about 150 miles east of Zamboanga. Our battalion boarded an LST on May 3rd and sailed across Moro Gulf to Parang, where we debarked the next day. The 24th Division had carried out an assault landing in the vicinity of Parang on April 17th. The 31st Division came ashore five days later; the area was secure when we arrived. The role of the 162nd Infantry was to serve as a reserve unit defending the beachhead, patrolling, and mopping up in the Cotabato area.

After several days, our 3rd Battalion and Battery C of the 205th Field Artillery Battalion were attached to the 24th Division, which was fighting in the vicinity of the city of Davao. The 24th Division had reached the Davao area by crossing Mindanao on Route 1 to Digos, situated on the Gulf of Davao about 20 miles south of the city of Davao. As we were preparing for the move to the Davao area, we received the news about the surrender of Germany. The news was encouraging, of course, but there was no celebration. The war was definitely not over for us; men were still dying in the jungles of the Pacific islands.

We boarded an LST that traveled southward around Tinaca Point, the southernmost tip of Mindanao, and then north into Davao

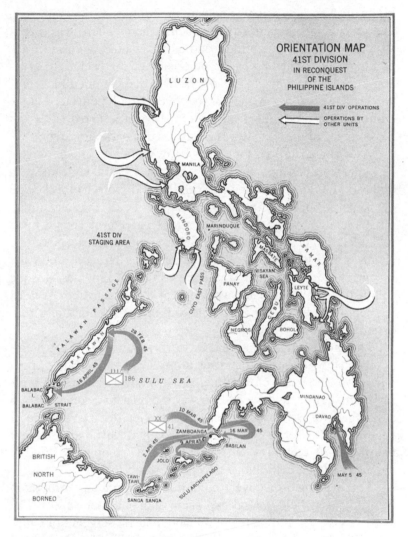

Orientation map, 41st Division in reconquest of the Philippine Islands.
From McCartney, *The Jungleers.*

Gulf. We landed at Digos and climbed aboard army trucks that traveled north toward Davao along Route 1, the same road that the troops of the 24th Division had taken as they made their advance toward Davao three weeks earlier.

The road that we traveled was a narrow two-lane concrete

highway. The Japs had blown up all the bridges as they retreated, and our engineers were busy replacing them. There was a construction delay at one bridge, and as we waited, an army truck coming south pulled up on the other side of the bridge. Its gruesome cargo was a load of dead GIs. The bodies, piled like cordwood on the bed of the truck, were covered with ponchos, but the combat boots protruding from under the cover left no doubt about the contents of the load. It was a sad and disheartening sight.

As we traveled along the road, we saw numerous groves of what I thought were banana trees. However, I never saw a single tree with any fruit. I assumed that the Nips and the Filipinos had picked all the bananas, but I could not understand why I didn't see any immature bunches of fruit. Several years after I had returned home, I was looking through a book that described trees when I saw a picture of an abaca tree. It looked just like a banana tree. The copy under the picture stated that the tree, which grew in the Philippines, was the source of Manila hemp and a relative of the banana tree. At last I learned why I had never been able to find any fruit on those "banana" trees.

The entire campaign around Davao is rather fuzzy in my memory, probably because most of us at my level really didn't know where we were most of the time. We had never operated as a reserve unit before, and we had no specific objectives other than to assist the 24th Division in their effort to clear the Davao area of enemy troops. We set up a perimeter south of Davao and sent out patrols for several days. Then members of Companies I and K climbed aboard trucks and headed back south.

That evening, as we were preparing to set up our perimeter in an open grassy field, a loud explosion rang out in our midst. The jeep carrying the company commander and 1st sergeant of Company K had hit a land mine, killing both men. The driver escaped with only a minor wound.

A short time later, we formed a line parallel to the edge of the road and slowly moved across the area, searching for other mines. The razor-sharp kunai grass in the field was about five feet tall, so we moved with great care as we advanced across the mined area. Most of us used sticks to part the grass before taking each step. The mines were actually buried bombs with only the noses sticking out of the ground. As each mine was found, its location was marked by driving a tall stick into the ground near the mine. The task was completed slowly and carefully without further mishap. I remember feeling that our hole that night was much too close to one of those buried bombs. I was happy when we moved out early the next morning.

That afternoon, we set up a perimeter and sent out patrols to scout the area. While our platoon was on a patrol, we discovered a small house that obviously had been occupied by the Japanese. There were Japanese books, pictures, bowls, and many other items in the house, but one thing in particular caught our attention. It was a small phonograph that was operated by manually winding a crank. On the table next to the phonograph was a large stack of records. One man picked up the phonograph; the rest of us took records. We carried our booty back to our perimeter, which was situated at the top of a high steep hill.

The phonograph was set up and wound. The first record was put on the turntable, and the characteristically tinny sound of Japanese music filled the afternoon air. After about half of the record had been played, someone took it off the turntable and threw it down the hill. A second record was put on the turntable. The same sequence of events took place. One by one, after a few bars of each had been played, the records were used as Frisbees and were sent sailing down the hill. Suddenly, we heard a female voice singing in English. The song was "My Blue Heaven." Shouts of approval rang out, and the record was played a second time. After the remainder of the records had been evaluated, our collection consisted of only one record, "My Blue Heaven," which I later learned was the favorite U.S. song of the Japanese at that time. Mercifully, after countless replays of the record, someone grabbed it and sent it to join the rest of the collection at the bottom of the hill. The phonograph shortly afterward suffered the same fate.

We shared the hill that night with two carabaos (water buffalo) that had been killed by mortar or artillery fire. Because we usually moved our perimeters every day, we did not bother to try to move the dead animals, even though their bodies were bloated and beginning to smell. The next day we sent out patrols, and instead of moving on, we returned to the same perimeter that afternoon. By then the stench of the decaying animals was intolerable; the carabaos had to be rolled down the hill. Because they were very large, probably weighing over 1,000 pounds each, it was a difficult and most disagreeable job. However, with a lot of pushing and tugging we were successful, and the odor within our perimeter quickly improved.

The next day while our platoon was on a patrol, Herb Santos shot and killed a wild boar. We carried the animal back to our perimeter, where it was hung from a tree and butchered by two of our farm boys, Stacy Wilson and Cliff Cole. We built a fire and roasted the pig. The animal was large enough to give most of the members of our platoon a small piece of meat. But we were all disappointed; the meat was tough and full of gristle.

We spent the last week of May in Santa Cruz, a small village south of Davao. Many of us attended Sunday Mass at the village church. After Mass we met a number of the parishioners, who were very happy to have us there and made every effort to make us feel welcome. Several of us talked to the parish priest, who told us that early in the war, when the Japs were nearing their village, he and the parishioners had taken his vestments and all the church furnishings —including the statues and the organ—up into the hills, where he hid from the Japs for over three years.

Most of the Filipinos we met spoke excellent English and related stories about the ill-treatment they had suffered at the hands of the Japanese. Most of them had been robbed of many of their possessions by the Japs but were happy, even eager, to share what they still had with us. I met a teenage Filipino girl, Aida Dean, who invited three of us to dinner at her parents' house. We accepted the invitation and that evening enjoyed a dinner of fish with rice. Dessert was fried bananas.

I also attended a party at the house of Charlie Perez, a very friendly young man. The high point of our stay was a dance held in the town meetingplace to which the entire company was invited. On the evening of the dance, the Filipinos, dressed in their best clothes, danced to the music of the village band. Although I didn't dance, I enjoyed just watching and listening.

We played two softball games against the Filipinos and won both of them, even though they did have a few very good players. In a letter to my sister I wrote, "I've enjoyed the past week more than any other since I've been overseas, Australia included." I was touched by many of the stories related to us by the Filipinos. In the same letter I wrote, "The longer I stay over here and the more I see of the Nips and their work, the more I hate them."

The next week was not nearly so pleasant for us. Our platoon was chosen to reinforce Company K in a series of landings to find and wipe out Japanese coast-watchers and their radio stations in the area around Davao Gulf. On the evening of May 31st, we embarked in a convoy of ten LCMs (landing craft mechanized) escorted by a destroyer, a destroyer escort, an LCIR, an LCIG (landing craft infantry, gunboat), and several PT boats. About 260 troops were being transported in the LCMs, which were flat-bottomed landing craft designed to land a medium tank or a large truck. The LCMs, fifty feet long and fourteen feet wide, were operated by Army Engineers. The cargo section of the LCM measured about 10 x 30 feet. About twenty-five men were being transported in those cramped quarters. There were no facilities for troops on the landing craft. Steel ribs ran across the bottom of the craft to furnish traction for trucks or other vehicles. To sleep, we had to lie on the ribbed steel bottom or sit upright against the sides of the LCM. There was no cover over our compartment; when it rained, we got soaked.

The next morning, after a miserable night, we stood offshore of Luayon, where our mission was to destroy a radio station. After a bombardment by our escort ships and an air strike, we landed against light opposition and accomplished our mission of destroying the radio station. Five Japanese were killed in the raid. We boarded our LCMs the same afternoon and made a landing the next morning at the village of Glan, which was held by Filipino guerrillas. On the morning of June 3rd, after another night in the LCMs, we made a landing at Balut Island at the southern end of Davao Gulf. We encountered opposition from the Japanese, pulled back, and boarded the LCMs again. The following day, we landed at a different point on the island and were able to find and destroy the radio station. Three Japs were killed during the raid.[1]

That afternoon, when we boarded our LCM for the voyage to our last objective, we encountered a problem. Our landing craft was

1. Morison, *The Liberation of the Philippines*, pp. 249–250.

stuck on the beach. The other LCMs had cleared the beach, but all efforts by the coxswain of our craft to move it were fruitless. We all debarked, but that did not help. Everyone climbed up onto the stern to try to raise the bow, but the LCM still could not move. With Lieutenant Armstrong giving signals, we jumped up and down in unison while the coxswain gunned the engine, trying to work the landing craft free. All efforts were in vain; our LCM was stuck.

It was getting dark, and the rest of the convoy departed. We were beached and remained so for almost an hour until the tide finally rose enough for the craft to be freed. It was completely dark by then, and we set out at full throttle in an attempt to rejoin the convoy. The LCM plowed through the water for a considerable length of time until suddenly, out of the darkness, a warship appeared abreast of us. The large ship was within 100 feet of our tiny craft, and we found ourselves staring at the business end of its big guns, which were aimed at us. It was the destroyer *Flusser,* which was furnishing cover for our convoy. Our LCM had been picked up on radar by the destroyer, whose crew assumed that we were an enemy craft. We learned that instead of being behind the convoy, we had passed it and were about a mile ahead of it. We were all very thankful that the skipper of the destroyer, Captain F. D. McCorkle, had waited for a positive identification before giving the order to fire.[2]

We arrived at our final objective, Cape San Augustin, on the morning of June 5th. Our landing on that morning was preceded by a bombardment. Before making a landing, I always put my wallet in my helmet liner so that it would not get wet if it was necessary to wade to shore. On that morning I was careless and did not take that precaution. When our LCM went in for the landing, it went aground on a sandbar about 100 yards offshore. We waded in water chest high. My pictures, money, and papers were soaked. We reached the beach with no further problems and encountered no opposition. Apparently, the Nips had retreated inland when the bombardment began. We were able to find and destroy several enemy installations, including a radio station, a fuel dump, and two generators.

That evening we reboarded our LCMs for the last leg of our journey, the return trip to Digos on the opposite side of Davao Gulf. Al-

2. Morison, *The Liberation of the Philippines,* p. 250.

though the Japs had not presented much opposition, it had been a very tiring and uncomfortable week. The nights on the LCM were awful. The hard, cold, ribbed-steel bottom of the craft made a very poor bed. We were exhausted, but as bad as the previous five nights had been, the worst was still to come.

Shortly after we had departed San Augustin the wind increased and the waves grew; soon we were in a tropical storm. Of course, the LCMs were not oceangoing vessels; they were not designed for smooth travel in rough waters. As the rain started and the wind grew stronger, our LCM rose out of the water and came down with a slap of its flat bottom against the waves. Each time the landing craft was thrown out of the water and hit the waves on its way back down, a shower of water descended on us.

After a short time, I began to get seasick. It was the first time I had suffered motion sickness since those first few days out of San Francisco. The sides of the LCM were about five feet high, so when the time came for me to get rid of my K-rations, I had to stand on my tiptoes to be certain my mouth cleared the side of the landing craft. Soon almost everyone was sick. The rain let up, but the splashing water kept us soaked. It was a miserable experience. I think one thing that helped me get through the night was a string of curse words coming from Smitty's mouth every time the LCM was thrown into the air and slammed back into the water. It was comforting to know that someone else was as miserable as I was.

When the long wretched night had ended and we were once more on dry land, it seemed like the ground was moving. I staggered to a dry spot on the beach and collapsed. I felt like the whole world was revolving around me. Mercifully, we were allowed to sleep on the beach most of that day. Late in the afternoon, we climbed aboard trucks for the drive to rejoin the rest of Company I.

We had only a few days to rest before we would be back in action again. It was during those days that we learned about the point system, a plan to determine the order by which servicemen and women would become eligible for discharge. At the time the plan was announced, anyone with eighty-five points or more would qualify. A point was awarded for every month of service and another for every month overseas; five points were awarded for each campaign star or combat decoration, such as the Combat Infantryman Badge or the

Purple Heart. Parents were credited with twelve points for each child, up to a maximum of three children. According to the plan, every original member of our division was eligible for discharge. However, only a small percentage of those eligible would be sent home each month. The first group to leave would be those men with the most points. Several members of our company were notified that they would start home on July 1st, which was only three weeks away. My point total was about fifty, so I knew that I was in for the duration of the war.

On June 10th, our battalion began a move to the front. The objective of the drive was the village of Calinan, northwest of Davao. We advanced along Route 1-D, a narrow unpaved road, without incident until the column stopped for a break. There was an abaca grove on one side of the road and an open field on the other. As I stood looking out across the open area, I saw a flash at the edge of the jungle beyond the field. The flash was instantly followed by the sound of exploding shells about twelve or fifteen yards to my right. I dove into a ditch along the roadside and heard the dreaded cry of "Medic!" ring out.

I was close to Lieutenant Armstrong, so I crawled over to him and told him that I had seen the muzzle blast of the artillery piece, probably a 75-mm cannon, that had fired on us. He pointed out an artillery observer who was accompanying us, and told me to give him the location of the enemy gun. The man was only about twenty feet from me, so I reached him quickly and pointed toward the area where I had seen the muzzle blast. He radioed his artillery and a round of fire landed near the spot I had pointed out. He asked me if the shells had landed in the right place. I told him to move the fire a little closer to us and slightly to the left. The second rounds fell very close to the area from which the Japanese gun had fired. After my nod of approval, the observer gave the order to fire for effect. We heard nothing more from the Nips or their gun. I had a feeling of power and satisfaction after directing the artillery fire on the Nips that afternoon. After the many times I had been on the receiving end of enemy fire, I very much enjoyed the opportunity to direct those artillery shells toward them.

We suffered fifteen casualties as a result of the enemy artillery fire; three men were killed. Among those killed was Robert Munson, one of the men who was scheduled to go home at the beginning of the next month. I believe that he had more points than anyone else in the regiment. The figure of 140 points sticks in my mind. I can still picture Ken Greene, with tears in his eyes, carrying his fallen buddy on his back. I can't recall the names of the other men who were killed, but one of those men was a young replacement seeing his first day of combat. All of us were saddened when anyone was killed, but I think everyone felt especially bad about Munson's death. We thought that he and the other men who were soon to go home should have been left behind when we moved out that morning.

We knew that every time we went into combat some of us would be killed, but I believe that most men thought that it would be someone else who would not come back. I never felt that I would be killed, but at times I did acknowledge that possibility. On those occasions, I always thought about how small the number of people was who would really care about my death. I knew that my immediate family and a small group of close friends and relatives would grieve for me, but I visualized other relatives, friends, and acquaintances saying, "What a shame! He was such a nice young man!" when they heard that I had been killed, but then rather quickly forgetting me. At those times I felt very insignificant in the grand scheme of things.

As the number of days that I spent in combat increased, thoughts about the law of averages crept into my mind more often. I became more apprehensive and, to some extent, more frightened each time we went into action. When I looked around at the men of our company, I could see that only a few of the original members were still with the company, and many of the men who had joined the company when I did were no longer with us. After sixteen months in the Southwest Pacific, I had become what the war correspondents referred to as a battle-hardened veteran.

In his book *A Soldier's Story,* General Omar Bradley addresses the plight of an infantryman subjected to repeated combat actions:

The rifleman trudges into battle knowing that statistics are stacked against his survival. He fights without promise of either reward or relief. Behind every river, there's another hill—and behind that hill, another river. After weeks or months in the line only a wound can offer him comfort of safety, shelter and a bed. Those who are left to fight, fight on, evading death but knowing that with each day of evasion they have exhausted one more chance for survival. Sooner or later, unless victory comes, this chase must end on the litter or in the grave.[3]

An incident occurred the following night that was particularly unnerving to me. Marty and I were asleep when a number of shots were fired from a foxhole to our right. All was quiet until a voice called out in Japanese from a position that was obviously very close to our perimeter. Then from the distance we could hear Japanese calling, apparently in answer. I expected that mortar or artillery fire would be forthcoming, but when nothing happened, I decided that the enemy soldier had been wounded and was calling for help. Apparently, the voices in the distance were those of his comrades who had not been wounded, at least seriously, by the fire from our perimeter and had withdrawn, leaving the wounded man. At intervals through much of the night the calls back and forth were repeated. Finally, all became quiet. Just before dawn we heard a muffled explosion. When daylight arrived we found the body of the Japanese soldier about sixty feet from our perimeter. He had exploded a grenade under his stomach. The dead Nip was not a pleasant sight.

We continued our advance. During the third week of June, the town of Calinan was captured, and we continued to move to the north in an effort to clear the Nips from that area. The thing I remember most vividly about the area was the mosquitoes. I carried a small bottle of insect repellent, but it was not very effective against those hungry devils. In an attempt to discourage the mosquitoes, I even resorted to smoking a cigarette or two. I remember preparing for sleep by rubbing the repellent on my face, neck, and hands. Then I buttoned my fatigue shirt to the neck, turned up the collar and put my fatigue cap on my head. I lay on my back in the foxhole, put a handkerchief over my face, and put my hands in my pockets. It was all to no avail. The mosquitoes would not be denied their evening meal.

Mistakes that are made during combat can, and often do, cost lives. Some mistakes cause what we refer to today as friendly fire

3. Bradley, *A Soldier's Story,* p. 321.

casualties. During the battles in which I took part, we were sub-jected to friendly fire from one of our planes on one occasion and from one of our ships on another. Because of the nature of jungle warfare, it was surprising that those types of mistakes did not hap-pen more often.

One day near the end of the Davao campaign, an incident oc-curred that demonstrated how easily serious and sometimes deadly mistakes can happen. As we were advancing along a road, we came under fire from a forested area bordering an abaca grove. An ob-server from our heavy mortar section who was accompanying us that day radioed instructions for a round of fire to be laid down on the target area; three rounds were fired, one from each mortar in the section. Two shells exploded on the target area; the third landed so close to us that I was showered with dirt. The observer angrily ordered the gunners to check their settings and fire by the numbers. The shells from the No. 1 and No. 2 mortars landed on target. The shell from the No. 3 mortar again landed much too close for comfort. Obviously, the setting on the No. 3 mortar was in error. I could not hear the conversation that took place between the observer and his section, but on the next round of fire, all shells hit the target area.

As we continued to advance, the enemy opposition lessened, and by the beginning of July we were encountering almost no op-position. One morning during the first week of July, I awakened, got out of my foxhole, and moved a short distance away to attend to my normal morning routine. Just as I finished relieving myself, I felt a severe pain in my lower right side and back. I made my way back to our foxhole where Marty was sitting. He could see that I was in pain and said, "What's wrong?" I told him what had hap-pened. He felt the painful area, and when the pain continued, he administered a shot of morphine. Marty told me to lie down and wait for an ambulance, which he would request for me. Our perim-eter was near the road, so I had only a short distance to walk when the ambulance arrived about fifteen minutes later.

The morphine was beginning to dull the pain as I got onto a stretcher in the ambulance. After a bumpy ride of fifteen or twenty minutes we reached the field hospital. By that time I was feeling much better. A doctor examined me and said that he thought I had a kidney stone. He told me to rest and said that he would see me again the next morning.

I spent the night on an army cot for the first time in two months. By the next morning I was feeling fine. The doctor came in and, after examining me, said that I had probably passed the stone. He told me that my outfit had been relieved shortly after I reached the hospital and would be leaving the area the next day. He said that if I wished, he would release me so that I could rejoin my company. I was happy to accept his offer; I was back with Company I that afternoon. The following day we boarded an LST for our return trip to Zamboanga.

U.S. casualties during the Davao campaign were listed as 820 killed and 2,880 wounded. The 41st Division losses were 25 killed and 85 wounded. When the campaign was officially closed, 10,540 Japanese were listed as killed.[4]

When we arrived at Zamboanga, we returned to the camp that we had set up two months earlier. Within the next few days I received a lot of mail, including some packages; saw the movie *National Velvet*; and enjoyed such treats as fresh eggs, chicken, and real hot dogs. Of course, it was always great to enjoy a good night's sleep under mosquito netting on a comfortable army cot. I was able to attend Mass and receive Communion. The war news continued to sound good; my morale was high.

I was back at my job in the supply room, where we were very busy. Replacement troops, who needed supplies and equipment, were arriving steadily. Some of the replacements who were coming from Europe were noncoms from air force ground crews and other noncombat units. The addition of the noncommissioned officers created problems within the company. The first problem was that these men were not infantrymen, and they lacked the training to serve as noncoms in a line infantry company. Also, the addition of these men brought the number of noncoms over the allotted number for the company. As a result of this troublesome situation, a number of combat veterans were acting as squad leaders or assistant squad leaders even though they were still privates. Those men often had one or more noncoms serving as riflemen under them in their squads.

4. Smith, *Triumph in the Philippines*, pp. 647–648.

As each day passed, the buildup continued for our next combat landing. We had no doubts about where the next fight would take place. It would be on the Japanese homeland. Anyone who had seen the fanaticism of the Japanese soldiers who defended those Pacific islands that were foreign to them could not look forward without considerable anxiety to fighting the Nips on their homeland. It would surely be a bitter and bloody battle.

During those days of preparation, I had a decision to make. The departure of the original members of the company continued, and their positions had to be filled. I was offered a choice of two jobs. The first offer was to become the armor artificer for the company. The second was to become a squad leader. The armorer's job carried a rating of T/5 (technical corporal); a squad leader was usually a staff sergeant. Given the situation on ratings at that time, it seemed that whichever position I chose I would remain a Pfc, at least for the immediate future.

I turned down the better potential rating of staff sergeant to become the company armorer. My job would be to maintain all the weapons in the company and to serve as assistant to the supply sergeant. The supply sergeant, Bernie Schimmel, and the armorer, Jack Williams, were on their way home. Jim Wood would be the new supply sergeant, and I would take over the armorer's job.

My first assignment was to attend a week of schooling that covered the operation and maintenance of all the weapons in the company. Of course, having carried an M1 rifle for more than two years, I was very familiar with that weapon, but in the company we also had carbines, .45-caliber hand guns, Thompson submachine guns, .30-caliber machine guns, 60-mm mortars, and bazookas. At the conclusion of the training, I returned to the company and began my new job.

The early days of August passed without incident until the afternoon of August 6th, when news spread through the camp that our air force had dropped an atomic bomb on Hiroshima, a city on Honshu, the largest Japanese island. I found the radio report of complete destruction of the city by one bomb hard to believe. I, like all of the other men, knew nothing about atomic bombs, so my first thought was that the extent of the damage had been exaggerated. It would not have been the first time we heard news reports that were badly biased in our favor. At Hollandia, when an enemy bombing attack destroyed most of our ammunition and supplies, our radio reports had described the damage as minor. On the second day of the Biak campaign, a news release issued by General MacArthur's headquarters proclaimed a victory that, in fact, took six more weeks to achieve. So I did not attribute to the news of the atomic bomb the significance that it deserved.

The report, two days later, of the Soviet Union's declaration of war against Japan was received with enthusiasm by everyone. It seemed now that the war might come to an end sooner than we expected, maybe even by Christmas. The next day, August 9th, we heard that a second atomic bomb had been dropped on Japan. The target was the city of Nagasaki. A great sense of excitement was beginning to build. Many of us gathered around radios and listened to the news. We heard reports of President Truman's broadcasts threatening Japan with destruction by atomic bombs unless they surrendered. Finally, the next night, August 10th, we heard that the Japanese Supreme War Council had agreed to accept the Potsdam Declaration and surrender, with the condition that the emperor be allowed to remain in power as the sovereign ruler.

The celebration began! Gunfire rang out both on land and at sea. Everyone was excited and very happy. Surely the war was all but officially over.

No one got much sleep that night. Small groups formed in the tents as we talked about returning to our families and homes. We all congratulated each other and consumed any booze that could be found. As the night wore on and the supply of liquor ran out, quiet was eventually restored. With feelings of hope, anticipation, and joy racing through my mind I was finally able to fall asleep.

For the next five days, I spent as much time as possible listening to news broadcasts. My new job as armorer made it possible to listen to the radio most of the day, and I stayed up until midnight every night listening to our radio in the supply tent. At last, on the morning of August 15th, we received the news we most wanted to hear: Emperor Hirohito announced in a radio broadcast to the Japanese people that Japan had accepted unconditional surrender. The war was over! August 15, 1945, was the long-awaited day. Because I had been taught by the Brothers of Mary at South Side Catholic High School, I was struck by the fact that, for the United States, the war had begun on December 8th, the day celebrating Mary's conception, and ended on August 15th, the feast of her assumption into heaven.

Strangely, there was not much celebration. We had done our celebrating five days earlier when we all assumed it would be only a short time until the war would be officially ended. I was excited and greatly relieved. I knew that if the war had not ended we would have been in battle with the Japanese on their homeland. I was not superstitious, nor did I have a foreboding about going into battle again, but I did know that the odds of going through a fifth major campaign unscathed were rather long.

After the war had ended, it was disclosed that the 41st Division would have been a part of the 650,000 man OLYMPIC Task Force to invade the southern Japanese island of Kyushu on D-Day, November 1, 1945. The invasion force would have been made up of fourteen U.S. divisions and supporting troops. The invading troops were to have been backed by 100,000 sailors and airmen. It would have been the largest amphibious operation in history, dwarfing the Normandy invasion. The Kyushu invasion was to have been followed three months later by the invasion of Honshu by the CORONET Task Force. Forty-two U.S. divisions under the command of General MacArthur were being readied to participate in the fight to destroy the Japanese Army, which still had several million men under arms. It was an army that had never lost a war over a period of 2,300 years.

Intelligence reports indicated that the Japanese anticipated the Kyushu invasion and were frantically building up their defenses for a fight to the death. Approximately 900,000 troops were on Kyushu when the war ended. About 3,300 army aircraft, including 2,100 kamikaze planes, and 5,225 navy planes, including 4,000 kamikaze aircraft, were positioned to defend against the invasion of Kyushu. Armored forces, including 488 tanks, were stationed on the island. Various suicide weapons, including midget submarines, motorboat bombs, human-swimmer bombs, attack boats, and human torpedoes were being readied. Kamikaze planes with detachable and reusable landing gear were being manufactured. Civilians were being trained and armed. Women, and even young boys, were being trained to fight using sharpened bamboo spears. The Japanese military leaders, believing that the gods would send a "divine wind" to save their homeland, were preparing to fight to the death. The leaders of the

Japanese military hoped that by inflicting such devastating casualties on the U.S. military, they could gain better terms of surrender. Undoubtedly, the invasion of Japan would have initiated a savage and merciless battle that would have resulted in the virtual destruction of the Japanese homeland.

U.S. casualties for the Kyushu landing were expected to be 250,000 men in the first sixty days. Estimates for U.S. casualties on the combined landings on Kyushu and Honshu ran as high as 1 million men.[5]

Japanese losses, both military and civilian, would have been staggering. The Japanese had 2 million troops, several million militia, and countless civilians ready to resist the U.S. landings and the Russian invasion. It has been estimated that as many as 20 million Japanese deaths would have resulted if an invasion had ended in a fight-to-the-death defense of the Japanese homeland.

I believe that those who still maintain that dropping the A-bomb was immoral should consider the cost in lives, both U.S. and Japanese, that would have been the result of an invasion of Japan. It is true that the atomic bomb dropped on Hiroshima killed about 100,000 Japanese, but it is also true that between 90,000 and 100,000 Japanese died as the result of an incendiary bomb raid on Tokyo by 279 U.S. planes that dropped 19,000 firebombs on the night of June 9, 1945.[6] It is difficult for me to understand why some consider it less moral to kill civilians with one atomic bomb than with thousands of firebombs.

I have no doubt that if the U.S. troops who were preparing for the invasion of Japan had been asked, they would have overwhelmingly approved the decision by President Truman to drop the atomic bombs. It was a decision that cost many Japanese their lives, but it was surely a decision that saved the lives of millions of Japanese and Americans, including, very possibly, my own.

While the war was still being fought, I, like most of the other men in our outfit, had a dual goal in mind—to survive and to go home with all body parts intact. Those of us with fewer than eighty-five points knew achieving that goal depended upon, among many things, the length of the war. We knew that unless we were seri-

5. Drea, *MacArthur's ULTRA*, pp. 217–222.
6. Harper, *Miracle of Deliverance*, p. 115.

ously wounded or killed, we would be fighting the Japanese until the day the war ended. When that happy day did arrive and our survival was assured, my attention was focused on a single goal—to go home. We who had fought and defeated the Japanese on the field of battle felt that we should receive some preference in the army's plan for returning troops to the U.S. We hoped that we would not have to rely solely on the point system to get home. All of us wanted our 41st Division to be sent home as a unit.

A few days after the Japanese surrender, I was doing some painting in the supply room when someone tapped me on the shoulder and said, "Hi, Bernie." I turned around to find Charlie Tichacek smiling at me. Charlie's home was only a few blocks from mine, and both of us had attended St. Pius School. He had been able to locate me because our parents had exchanged information about us and our outfits. We discussed old times, the whereabouts of mutual friends, and our travels and adventures during the war. One discouraging fact came out in an otherwise enjoyable meeting. Charlie was a ground crew member of an air squadron. He had seen no combat whatsoever, and in fact had never seen a Japanese soldier, but he had three battle stars. I had been in four major campaigns and had only two battle stars, one for New Guinea and one for the Philippines. It was the beginning of my disillusionment and disappointment with the point system. The battle stars were each worth five points in compiling the scores that were being used to determine the order by which we were to be discharged.

As the remainder of August passed, we waited for word on the immediate future of the 41st Division. Most of us expected that our next move would take us to Japan, but there were rumors that the division would be going home. On September 2nd, V-J Day, we listened to reports of the formal surrender ceremonies aboard the *USS Missouri*. We also heard that the advance elements of U.S. occupation troops had landed in Japan with no problems.

General MacArthur announced on September 10th that the 41st Division would occupy the Kure-Hiroshima area on the island of Honshu. Preparations began immediately for the move to Japan. It was a busy time in the supply room as we began to ready our equipment for the move. We were to be fully equipped for combat as we embarked for what we hoped would be a peaceful landing.

8

Japan
Army of Occupation

On September 19th, the members of our battalion boarded a troop transport, part of a twenty-ship convoy that departed later that afternoon for Japan. After two days at sea, we arrived at Leyte, where we spent a day in the bay while supplies were taken aboard. The next morning the convoy departed Leyte, resuming the voyage to the Japanese homeland. We arrived at Okinawa on September 25th, where the convoy anchored in Buckner Bay.

After the convoy had been anchored in the bay for two days, we learned that a typhoon was heading for Okinawa. There were ships of every description in the harbor at that time, but within a few hours most of them departed, heading for the open sea in an attempt to flee the path of the typhoon. Later that afternoon, our convoy pulled anchor and headed out to sea. We were told nothing about the direction from which the typhoon was approaching, so I assumed that we were heading for Japan. However, when I went on deck the next morning, although there were clouds in the sky, I could tell that the sun was rising directly over the stern of the ship; we were heading west toward the coast of China. We continued on our westerly course throughout the day. The next morning, the ship was heading directly into the sun. We had reversed our course during the night. The convoy continued on its eastward course until we arrived back at Buckner Bay that afternoon.

We had traveled through some very rough water the two previous days. The waves in the East China Sea were by far the highest I had ever seen, but I stayed on deck most of the time and did not suffer from motion sickness at all. I had become a reasonably good sailor. Our second visit to Okinawa lasted only a few hours. Late that afternoon we departed again, headed for Japan. When I went up on deck the next morning, I could not believe my eyes. The sun was on the port side of the ship; we were heading south. That afternoon we arrived at a place that was becoming quite familiar, Buckner Bay. I assumed that we were still trying to dodge storms, but we learned later that the delay was caused by slow progress in clearing mines from the Inland Sea of Japan. We spent two days in the bay before departing Okinawa for the third time on October 3rd.

The next morning the sun was on the correct side of the ship and remained so until the shoreline of the land we were about to occupy came into view. From a distance, the island of Honshu looked much like many other Pacific islands, like the tip of a big mountain rising from the sea. As we came closer, we could see steep cliffs rising from the shore. Small villages and tiny hillside farms were visible. It was very beautiful, but we could also see caves in the shoreline cliffs, and many of them were sealed by metal doors facing seaward. Those caves obviously housed shore batteries. This would have been far from an ideal spot to make an assault landing.

Our convoy arrived in the Kure area during the afternoon of October 6th. It had taken 18 days to make the trip from the Philippines to Japan. The harbor at Kure was an excellent one, but it was literally filled with Japanese warships ranging in size from battleships to midget submarines. The Japanese had been instructed to assemble all of their remaining warships in the harbor at Kure, and they had done so. A later count listed a total of 149 warships in the harbor; 106 were listed as serviceable. Because there were so many Japanese ships in the harbor, we were forced to transfer to LCVPs (landing craft vehicles and personnel) to make our landing. We loaded into the landing craft by descending on rope netting hung over the side of our transport. It was the first time we made a landing in that manner.

As we circled in the small boats, a feeling of uneasiness came over me. I could see Japanese sailors lining the rails of the large warships far above our small craft. It may have been unreasonable, but my thoughts went back to the many Japanese soldiers who, although hopelessly trapped, would never surrender. It was difficult for me to believe that all those Japanese on all those ships were surrendering so meekly. I was not at all happy with the thought of sailing between those enemy warships in our tiny landing craft.

Our leaders had more faith in the enemy than I, because we headed for shore, wending our way between the warships with the enemy sailors looking down at us as we looked up at them. "I'm going to be mad," I thought, "if after getting through almost two years of combat without a scratch, I am killed by the Nips after the war has ended."

My fears proved to be groundless; we reached the beach without incident. Two unarmed Japanese officers waiting on the shore saluted as we stepped ashore. A short discussion took place between our officers and the Japanese. Either the Japanese could speak English or a Nisei interpreter accompanied our officers. An understanding was reached quickly, and we immediately began to march toward our destination, a submarine base along the shore of the bay.

As we marched through the city, the streets were deserted except for Japanese policemen wearing blue uniforms and carrying shiny swords. The policemen, who were stationed at the intersection of each side street, stood at attention facing away from us, which, I learned later, was a sign of respect and honor according to Japanese custom. Every three or four blocks there was a small booth manned by Japanese soldiers who stood at attention and saluted as we passed. The windows of many of the buildings along the streets were boarded up, but occasionally we could see someone peeking out at us. There was an eerie silence as we marched through the city. The situation seemed unreal to me. I had difficulty believing that after so much violent and bitter fighting we were so quietly and peacefully occupying the Japanese homeland.

When we reached the base after a march of about two miles, we found many of the buildings damaged and very dirty. The first order of business was to clean and treat the buildings with DDT to kill the fleas that were prevalent. The weather was so cool that I could see my breath. It really felt cold to me after such a long time in the tropical climates of New Guinea and the Philippines. We were dressed in summer fatigues; winter-weight uniforms were not available until several weeks later. To further our discomfort, rain started to fall on the first afternoon and continued for the next four or five days.

On the second day, a few children began to appear on the streets. When some of the GIs gave candy or gum to the children, all of us became their friends very quickly. After another day or two, adult Japanese started to appear. By the end of the first week, the streets were crowded; everything went well. Some of the Japanese seemed frightened; others tried to be friendly.

Jim Wood and I set up the supply room, which also doubled as our bedroom. It seemed strange but nice to be sleeping in a building again. It was the first time I had done so since leaving the United States. The building did not have any heat, though, and we were right on the waterfront, where there was a very cool breeze most of the time.

Shortly after our arrival, everyone received flu shots. I was sick for a day or two afterward. Before and after any move, the supply room is always a busy place, so I did not have time to see much of the city. I did see some areas, though, that were completely burned to the ground. Large factories had been located in those burned-out sections. Apparently our bombers had been very accurate, because most of the nearby houses suffered only slight damage.

After every move, there was always a period of time with no incoming mail. The move to Japan was no exception. For most of us, no mail meant low morale. I am certain that most of those at home did not realize how much receiving a letter meant to us who were so far away from home. My immediate family was so faithful in writing to me that when I did not receive any mail I blamed the army's mail system. However, at times I became angry at some of my friends, usually without just cause, when I felt that too much time had elapsed since I had received a letter from one of them. I very much wanted to go home, and until that time would come, a letter from someone at home was the next best thing to being there.

The food that we had been eating since we arrived in Japan was another reason why our spirits were low; we were living exclusively on C-rations that had been packed in Australia three years previously. In a letter to my mother, I wrote, "I guess they have a lot of that junk stacked up on the islands and the only way they can get rid of it is to feed it to us. I get more disgusted with this Army every day, but the end of the trail is in sight now."

The loudest complaints of all, though, were those caused by the announcements about discharges. We heard that anyone in the United States with at least two years of service would be eligible for immediate discharge. We who had been in combat zones that long would have to wait. Then we heard the news that anyone thirty-five years of age or older would be eligible for discharge. We saw men who had just come overseas going back home. Many of them were fathers who spent most of the war in the states. It seemed that everyone but GIs of my age with a measly fifty-five points had an angle to get out of the army. My buddies and I spent hours cursing the army and the point system. The morale of our outfit, which had been surprisingly high during the war, was deteriorating as we carried out the occupation of the enemy homeland. We continued to hold out faint hope that the 41st Division would be sent back to the United States as a unit. We had lived and fought together, and we felt that we deserved the recognition of going home together. Instead, the 41st was being torn apart. All that we could do was wait and curse our fate.

After the rainy first week of our stay, the weather improved. The nights were cool, but the days were sunny and comfortable, very much like October weather in St. Louis. Radio reports told about the damage on Okinawa caused by the typhoon that had forced us to take evasive action. We also heard reports that the 41st Division would be available for return to the United States in December, but we had heard so many rumors about that subject since the war's end that I did not have high hopes that it would take place.

The Japanese people, especially the women and children, were becoming friendly. The mail had started to arrive, but the chow was still very disappointing. We continued to exist primarily on the awful Australian C-rations. During our free time, some of us played softball for entertainment. It was the only exercise that I was getting at the time. On most days, I was busy in the supply room. During the evening hours I stayed in the barracks. I did not trust the Japanese enough to roam the streets at night. I had no interest in sightseeing; I just wanted to go home.

About two weeks after our arrival at Kure, I was able to get a ride on an army truck to Hiroshima; it was a trip of about fifteen miles. The area was being occupied by units of the 41st Division. I had talked to other GIs who had seen the ruins and heard their descriptions of the devastation, but I was still amazed and shocked when I saw the utter destruction with my own eyes. When I stood at the center of the blast area near the Aioi Bridge, which had been the aiming point for the bomb, I could look in any direction, and the only buildings I could see standing were several stone or concrete structures that looked as if they might collapse at any moment. The smaller buildings were absolutely leveled. Metal safes and heating radiators were the only things that were not destroyed. The few automobiles and trucks that I saw were smashed as if a large, heavy object had fallen on them. The Ota River and its tributaries that flowed through the city had not served as barriers to the firestorm; the destruction on one side of the rivers was identical to that on the other. Trees and telephone poles were upright, but they were burned black. There was not a green leaf or a blade of green grass in the city.

While I walked among the ruins, I noticed a few Japanese picking through the rubble. One man came up to me, pointed to the sky, held up one finger, and then pointed to the wasteland around us. The city of Hiroshima had not been bombed prior to the dropping of the atomic bomb, so the fact that a single bomb could wreak such terrible desolation left the Japanese in a state of fear and disbelief.

As souvenirs of that historic event, I picked up three ceramic teapot lids that had been fused by molten glass that had flowed over them. I also took a small ceramic candleholder that had been softened and misshaped by the intense heat of the atomic explosion. After taking several photographs with my little Brownie camera, I boarded the truck and returned to Kure with mixed feelings. I felt sorrow and pity for the victims of the bomb, but I was convinced that if the bomb had not been dropped the war would still be in progress. I was happy and thankful that the carnage had ended. Undoubtedly, the results of an invasion of Japan would have been devastating for the Japanese people and extremely costly in lives lost for the U.S. forces involved.

After about three weeks at Kure, we received word that we would be moving to a different location. Preparations were begun for yet another move. On October 28th, everyone in our company except me climbed aboard army trucks to move to Fukuyama, a town on the Inland Sea fifty-seven miles east of Kure. I remained behind with the barracks bags, the supplies, and the extra weapons that were not taken on the trucks with the rest of the company. I was instructed to wait until a truck arrived that would take me and the supplies to Fukuyama.

After a short wait, instead of a U.S. truck that I was expecting, a rather decrepit Japanese army truck pulled up. Two Japanese soldiers got out and approached me. They bowed to me and began loading the supplies onto their truck. I presume that neither of the men could speak English; I certainly could not speak Japanese. Not a word was uttered as they loaded the truck. When the rest of our company left earlier, it had not occurred to me that I would be riding alone with a pair of Japanese soldiers through the countryside to a town whose name I had never heard until the previous day. I was not happy about being put into what was to me a most undesirable situation.

When the two men finished loading the truck, they bowed to me and climbed into the front seat of the truck. Grabbing my trusty M1 rifle, which was fully loaded, I climbed atop the barracks bags, and the truck slowly and rather noisily pulled away. It was a sunny and very comfortable afternoon, and under different circumstances I would have thoroughly enjoyed my ride. The countryside was scenic. Small farmhouses surrounded by vegetable gardens dotted the landscape. The crops were growing on every square inch of soil, including the shoulders of the road. In the distance to the north, mountains were visible. Occasionally, I could catch a glimpse of the Inland Sea to the south.

As we drove along, the road led us through several very small villages. The streets were so narrow and the houses were so close to the street that the sides of the truck almost touched the overhanging roofs. Some of the Japanese gave me quizzical looks; others looked up and then quickly turned away. We seemed to be traveling in the right direction, and as our journey continued without incident, my apprehension lessened. Soon we arrived at a site on the shore of the Inland Sea on which barracks buildings and airplane hangars were located. The truck pulled up to one of the buildings and stopped. I quickly climbed down from my perch atop the barracks bags. The driver and his cohort again bowed to me and began to unload the truck. I acknowledged their bows by nodding before heading into the barracks to investigate our new quarters.

The site that we would now occupy was a seaplane base located about five miles from the outskirts of Fukuyama. The buildings appeared to be almost brand-new. Our barracks was in excellent condition. There were several hangars, some of them still under construction. The hangars were filled with seaplanes and bombs. During the next several weeks, our job would be to destroy the planes and dispose of the bombs and any other ammunition at the base. The buildings were in a rural area close to the waterfront. I liked our new quarters much better than those at Kure.

As the days passed, the weather became colder. At last we received winter clothing, which we issued to the members of the company. The job of destroying the planes was proceeding, but I was not involved; Jim Wood and I were very busy in the supply room. The planes were being destroyed by towing them out to sea, where they were sunk by detonating explosives attached to the pontoons of the planes.

Rumors continued to circulate. The latest rumor had the 41st Division leaving December 2nd to return to Seattle on December 18th. Two men from the St. Louis area, Orville Alexander and Richard Jones, left during the week. Orville was eligible because of his age, and Richard had seventy-nine points. Both of the men joined Company I about a month after I had. The point system continued to function, but not without some glitches. One day we said goodbye to the guys with seventy-three points and over, only to see them return a week later. The ship on which they were scheduled had been sent to China to pick up some marines. The men who returned were in a foul mood, but a few days later they left for the second time; we never saw them again.

The days moved by very slowly for most of us, but we were now into the third week of November. One day the mail clerk came into our little supply room carrying seven packages, three for Jim and four for me. They were Christmas packages that had arrived in perfect condition and in record time. The outlook for chow improved dramatically with the receipt of those goodies.

One afternoon I went into the town of Fukuyama to do some

shopping at a bazaar. I was hoping to buy some items to send home as Christmas presents. I came back to our quarters empty-handed and angry. It seemed to me that the Japanese were already beginning to take advantage of us. The prices that they were asking were much higher than I was willing to pay. In a letter to my mother I wrote, "You'd think that the Nips had won the war instead of us."

In the opinion of lowly GIs such as I, the army did a lot of dumb things. On the day before Thanksgiving, one such incident took place. Each man was given a fifth of whiskey, a bottle of sake, and a case of beer. I could not believe that we would be issued that much liquor at one time. I knew that there would be a few men who would try to drink it all the first night. It was indeed a wild night. Among the many events that took place was a football game in the mess area with a turkey being used as the football by the cooks. I traded my bottle of whiskey for a large silk Japanese flag and my sake for a pretty blue silk kimono. The case of beer kept me in booze for about two weeks.

The Thanksgiving dinner left something to be desired. In a letter to my sister, I related the sequence of events, "We had turkey without trimmings on Thanksgiving, then today all the trimmings arrived, so tomorrow we'll have trimmings without turkey. That's the army for you."

On the day after Thanksgiving we were entertained by a small orchestra of Japanese musicians and five geisha girls who sang and danced. The women were dressed in long silk kimonos and wore heavy white makeup. The orchestra played soulful Japanese melodies as the geisha girls danced slowly while singing in Japanese. Most of those in attendance were not enthusiastic about the evening's entertainment, but the performers were rewarded with polite applause when the show ended.

During the week after Thanksgiving, a big recruiting drive was held. A surprising number of men signed up. Most of them were young soldiers with eight or ten points who had just arrived in Japan from the United States. They were promised furloughs to go home for Christmas as incentives to re-enlist. This angered those among us who were waiting for space aboard ships. Those men who re-enlisted would push us farther down the list of those waiting for ships home.

I did receive a pleasant surprise early in December: I was promoted to the rank of T/5. Enough noncoms had gone home to allow me to receive the rating, which increased my salary by $15 per month. My new MOS of 511 identified me as an armor artificer.

Shortly after that, I heard an announcement on the radio that anyone with fifty-five points or more was eligible for discharge. Although I was now eligible, I knew that there would still be a wait because men with as many as sixty-eight points were still waiting for word to ship out.

During that first week of December, I received a torn and battered package from home that was postmarked July 7th. It had been en route for five months and looked it. I was able to salvage only a roll of film and two packages of licorice. In answer to a letter from my mother asking what I would like for Christmas I wrote, "If you want to get me a Christmas present, a watch or a wallet would be fine. I'm afraid both my watch and wallet have been in too much salt water. Any kind of watch would be O.K., just so it looks nice and isn't a military style." I very much wanted to be a civilian again.

As the days passed, we continued to collect many Japanese weapons. Most of the war materiel was destroyed, but we were allowed to keep a few items for souvenirs. Everyone who had earned the Combat Infantryman Badge received a silk scarf made to be worn by the Japanese kamikaze pilots. I also was able to choose a rifle from a large pile of weapons that had been gathered. I chose what appeared to be a brand-new model 44 carbine. It was a weapon that I had never seen before. It was shorter than the standard Japanese rifle and carried a built-in triangular-shaped bayonet that folded under the barrel of the rifle when it was not in use. The carbine used 6.5-mm ammunition. I boxed the rifle and sent it home; it hangs in my den as a reminder of those difficult days many years ago.

Two of my best friends, Sal Ferrara and Martin Lee, left for home on December 5th. Both men had been wounded at Zamboanga; each had sixty-three points. I was happy for them, but I was also saddened by their departure.

In a letter to my Aunt Vi dated December 12, 1945, I wrote, "This is not going to be much of a letter because I'm so excited I can't sit still. The fifty-nine pointers left today and the fifty-eights were just alerted to leave tomorrow. Jim Wood and Stacy Wilson will be among those who will be going home. I'm sweating out each day. I know that I shouldn't be getting so excited, but seeing all the guys I've been with for so long going home is just getting the best of me. It's no use trying to write any more."

9

The Long Journey Home

At long last the day for which I had been waiting arrived. It was December 22, 1945. Along with eleven other members of Company I, Smitty and I boarded a train at the station in Fukuyama. We settled in our seats for what was to be an eighteen-hour ride to Nagoya, our port of embarkation.

Shortly after our departure, an incident occurred that demonstrated how some Japanese felt about U.S. soldiers. A GI sitting in the seat in front of me was reading a magazine in which there was an advertisement for a war movie. A photograph in the ad showed an American soldier strangling a Japanese soldier. The conductor of the train, a middle-aged bespectacled Japanese man dressed in a black uniform and cap, noticed the picture as he walked down the aisle. Smiling, he pointed to the Japanese soldier in the photo and said, "Chinaman." When the GI told the conductor that it was a Japanese soldier, he became very upset and said, "No, no, Chinaman, Chinaman." He turned away and hurriedly left the car. It seemed inconceivable to me that for almost four years we had been mortal enemies, and now only four months after the end of the war, this man wanted so badly to be accepted as our friend that he was trying to deny that we had ever been enemies.

The next day we arrived at Nagoya, where another countdown began. My third Christmas away from home passed almost without

notice. There were no religious services, nor was there any other ac-
knowledgement of Christmas. We were housed in a huge bare building furnished with nothing but closely spaced army cots. There was
nothing to do but wait. The weather was cold and rainy. Time seemed
to stand still. After six incredibly long days, my name appeared on a
list of men scheduled to embark the next day. On the morning of December 29th, I boarded the troop transport *USS Admiral H. T. Mayo*
to begin the long-awaited voyage to San Francisco. The *Admiral
Mayo* was by far the best ship on which I had ever traveled. The chow
was reasonably good and the weather was fine, but the days just
dragged. As on most ocean voyages there was not much to do but
read, play cards, or watch the waves. I spent most of my time sitting
on deck doing nothing but thinking, watching, and waiting.

On December 31, 1945, two days after I had boarded the ship for
my voyage home, the 41st Division was deactivated, and the men
still with the division were assigned to other outfits. It seemed to me
that it was a sad and inglorious end for a proud veteran division. The
41st had been called into federal service on September 16, 1940. The
deactivation ended a period of active service of five years, three
months, and fifteen days. The 41st Division was the first division to
go overseas during World War II and spent three years and ten
months overseas before its deactivation.

Members of the division participated in the campaigns for Papua
New Guinea, Dutch New Guinea, and the southern Philippines and
took part in assault landings at Nassau Bay, Hollandia, Aitape,
Wakde-Arare-Toem, Biak, Palawan, Zamboanga, Sanga Sanga,
Sulu Archipelago, and Jolo. More than 1,000 members of the division lost their lives in battle. More than 4,400 men were wounded in
action. The Japanese lost more than 24,000 men in their battles
against the 41st Division. The division was one of the most experienced and most highly regarded divisions in the Pacific Theater.

In an inspection of the division at Zamboanga on June 15,
1945, General MacArthur wrote:

> Everything is as I expected to see it, in splendid shape. This is one of my
> oldest and proudest divisions. Its achievements have been of the first or-
> der. I have the greatest affection for and pride in the 41st Division.[1]

---

1. McCartney, *The Jungleers,* Foreword.

New Year's Day came and passed, but the next day we crossed the international date line and had the opportunity to celebrate the new year again. The voyage continued without incident as the ship plowed steadily through the waves on its easterly course until, on the morning of the eighth day, I noticed by observing the position of the sun that we were heading in a southerly direction. I knew that we were not going to reach San Francisco on the course we were following at that time. I was concerned, and I wondered what had happened to cause us to change course.

Later in the day we learned that a man aboard ship had suddenly become seriously ill. We had altered our course to take him to the nearest hospital, which was in Hawaii. The next afternoon we arrived at Pearl Harbor; the sick GI was taken ashore, and we resumed our voyage to San Francisco. Even though we were all very eager to get home, I am reasonably certain that no one objected to the detour, which delayed our arrival at San Francisco by three days.

Early on the morning of January 10, 1946, the long-awaited sight of the California shoreline came into view. It had been twenty-three months and five days since I departed San Francisco aboard the *USAT Sea Corporal*. The closer we came to shore, the more excited I became. The fact that I would soon be walking on U.S. soil seemed almost too good to be true.

Later that morning I could see the Golden Gate Bridge in the distance. It was almost exactly noon when the ship went under the bridge. We were escorted by a yacht that carried a band and ten or twelve pretty girls on the top deck. The girls waved and the band played. As we moved slowly into San Francisco Bay, all the ships in the harbor began sounding their horns and whistles to greet us. I had a lump in my throat; I wasn't crying but my eyes were getting watery. I was happy beyond words.

By the time we docked, I had regained my composure. We debarked and immediately boarded a ferry, which took us up the bay to Camp Stoneman at Pittsburg, California. We were checked in, assigned bunks, and then treated to the best meal I had eaten since leaving the United States. It was a steak dinner complete with salad, French fries, fresh vegetables, and ice-cold milk. For dessert I had cake, ice cream, and a Coke. I enjoyed all the food, but I particularly liked the green salad, the ice cream, and the cold milk.

That evening I enjoyed my first hot shower in almost two years. It was really a treat; I stayed in the shower for a long time. It was also great to sleep on a bed with a mattress that night. That, too, was a first since leaving the United States. Before I went to sleep, I thanked the good Lord for my safe return and for His many blessings. With happy thoughts racing through my mind, I quickly fell asleep in my soft, dry, clean bed.

The next morning I was told that it would probably be three or four days until a troop train would be available for the trip to Jefferson Barracks, where I was to be discharged. Until that time arrived I had nothing to do but eat, sleep, think about the events of the past two and a half years, and make plans for the immediate future.

That night I wrote my last letter to my mother to let her know that I had arrived in California safely and that I should be home in about ten days. In my letter I mentioned that I had figured out how much time I had spent at sea. According to my calculations, the total was ninety-nine days. I found it ironic that I spent that much time at sea, because on the day of my induction I was given a choice of service in either the army or the navy. I was a midwestern city boy who had never seen an ocean, so I chose the army.

Two of my friends, Phil Kratzert and Bob Park, who were being examined the same day, chose the navy and urged me to do the same. I declined because I was afraid that I would not like life aboard ship. I was sworn into the army that day, but Phil and Bob were sent to the Federal Building, where they were reexamined by the navy. Bob passed his physical and was sworn in, but Phil was rejected because of a punctured eardrum. The next day he was reexamined by the army and rejected, even though it had passed him the previous day. Phil then volunteered for service in the merchant marine, but he was turned down. He spent the war as a civilian, but if he had chosen the army that day, he would have been sworn in with me.

I questioned my choice of the army on more than one occasion, especially when I could see ships offshore and visualize the sailors wearing clean uniforms, eating hot meals, and sleeping in dry, comfortable bunks while I sat in the rain in a muddy foxhole and ate K-rations.

As I looked back, though, I knew that I had made the right choice because the experiences of combat and the hardships I had endured would favorably affect the way I would live the rest of my life. It had been a difficult thirty-one months. I did not feel that I had done anything heroic or extraordinary; nevertheless, I was proud of what I had accomplished. I was still only 21 years old, but I had matured and gained a lot of confidence in my ability to cope with any problems that I might encounter in the future. I had traveled over 30,000 miles during my army career, taken part in four major campaigns, and participated in eight assault landings. I estimated that I spent about 170 nights sleeping in foxholes. I had suffered malaria, hepatitis, jaundice, dysentery, and jungle rot, but had not missed a day of combat. I gave thanks to the good Lord for my safe passage through the many days and nights of danger.

Now, more than fifty years later, as I reflect on the war and the part I played in it, I am glad that it was World War II and particularly the war against Japan in which I took part. The great majority of us who participated felt that it was our duty and would have been disappointed if we had not been able to serve. We had suffered a sneak attack at the hands of the Japanese and felt we had to defend ourselves. The entire country was united in an all-out effort to win the war. There were no doubts about justification in our minds as we fought and killed the Japanese. It was a merciless kill-or-be-killed war, and the fact that the Japanese were almost never willing to surrender gave us no choice but to destroy them, usually to the last man.

As a member of a military unit whose sole mission during the war was to search out and destroy the Japanese, I willingly played an active role in the killing of the enemy. On one occasion I directed artillery fire which almost certainly killed a number of Japanese. On another day when Stacy Wilson and I were the lead scouts, we spotted a small group of Japanese who were all killed within a few minutes by machine-gun fire from our weapons platoon. There were other occasions when I, with other members of the company, returned fire into the jungle at the hidden enemy; however, I am not certain that a bullet fired from my rifle ever killed an enemy soldier. I know that I share with my fellow soldiers the responsibility for the deaths of many Japanese; killing the enemy was our job. Nevertheless, I am thankful that I was spared the experience of knowing that I had personally killed a fellow human being by firing a bullet into his head or plunging a bayonet into his belly. War, especially for the infantryman, is a brutal, ugly, and merciless endeavor.

Even so, I am proud that I served in the infantry, "The Queen of Battle." I am proud of the division, the regiment, and particularly the company in which I served. Men who lived and fought together as infantrymen (or dogfaces, as we were sometimes called) developed feelings of friendship and respect for each other that cannot be easily explained to anyone who has not experienced the hardships and the terror of combat. I regret that I did not maintain those relationships over the years since the end of the war; but as I write about those happenings of years past, I am looking forward to attending my first Company I reunion in Bend this summer. As I look back, I am certain that Company I was the "good spot" in the U.S. Army that had been promised to me on my first day of active service.

On January 12th, I learned that I would board the train to St. Louis the next morning. My excitement had subsided by the time I climbed aboard the train. I knew it was only a matter of a few days until my army career would come to an end. The days during the trip seemed very long, but at last, on the morning of January 17th, the train pulled onto a siding at Jefferson Barracks. The discharge process began immediately.

I can recall very little about the proceedings. Of course, there was a physical exam. My weight was 127 pounds. I had lost 23 pounds during the two years overseas. There were lectures and interviews in which the advantages of army life were stressed. We were asked individually if we wanted to re-enlist or be discharged. The answer was easy for me. I had already decided that after my discharge, I would use the GI Bill to enroll at St. Louis University with the intention of obtaining a degree in engineering.

Those who chose to be discharged received a Separation Qualification Record, which was to be presented to prospective employers as an aid in finding employment as civilians. My form listed my military occupations as rifleman and armorer. Under the heading of rifleman, the form read as follows: "In an infantry rifle company fired semi-automatic rifle during combat operations against the enemy. Also used hand grenades during combat. Received advanced combat infantry training." Under the heading of armorer the form read as follows: "Repaired and maintained semi-automatic and au-

tomatic rifles, mortars, bazookas, machine guns, pistols and carbines." Under the heading of Military Education the word "None"
was the only entry. My feeling at that time was that the form would
not be of much help in finding civilian employment.

Each of us received a form signed by President Harry S Truman thanking us for our service to the nation. At last, on the morning of January 18, 1946, after two years, six months, and twenty-
eight days of service I received my Honorable Discharge from the
Army of the United States. I was entitled to $300 mustering-out
pay, but I received only $100 at the time of separation. The balance
was to be paid in two monthly payments of $100 each. Because I
had never been granted a furlough during my entire time in service, I was entitled to furlough pay based on thirty days per year of
service. I was also entitled to 65 cents travel pay. I signed the pay-
roll and received $217.83 from the disbursing officer.

My discharge papers listed "Convenience of the Government"
as reason for my separation. Under the heading "Battles and Campaigns," New Guinea and Southern Philippines were listed. My
service entitled me to wear the Combat Infantryman Badge, the
Bronze Star Medal, the Asiatic-Pacific Campaign Medal with two
Bronze Stars and a Bronze Arrowhead, the American Campaign
Medal, the World War II Victory Medal, the Good Conduct
Medal, the Army of Occupation Medal with Japan Clasp, the Meri-
torious Unit Emblem, the Philippine Liberation Ribbon with one
Bronze Star, the World War II Honorable Service Lapel Button,
and three Overseas Bars.

However, I did not receive any of the medals or campaign ribbons except the Combat Infantryman Badge until about fifty years
later. With the exception of that badge, which I had received at
Biak, my uniform was bare. I did not have my stripes, the 41st Division shoulder patch, or even the blue braid of an infantryman on
my cap. As I walked down the street toward the bus stop at Jefferson Barracks with my overcoat covering my Combat Infantryman
Badge, I could have been mistaken for a brand-new buck private.
But I did not care; I was very happy. I carried my barracks bag over
my shoulder and an envelope with my discharge papers in my
hand. My service in the Army of the United States had been
completed.

After a short wait I boarded the Barracks bus, transferred to the Broadway streetcar and then to the Chippewa bus. I got off the bus at the northeast corner of Chippewa and Arkansas, hoisted my barracks bag to my shoulder, and, as was fitting for a foot soldier, began to walk the last half block of my long journey home.

BIBLIOGRAPHY

Barbey, Daniel E. *MacArthur's Amphibious Navy*. Annapolis, Md.: United States Naval Institute, 1969.
Bergerud, Eric. *Touched with Fire: The Land War in the South Pacific*. New York: Viking Press, 1996.
Bradley, John H. *The Second World War: Asia and the Pacific*. West Point Military History Series, vol. II. Wayne, N.J.: Avery Publishing Group, 1989.
Bradley, Omar N. *A Soldier's Story*. New York: Henry Holt & Company, 1951.
Craven, Wesley Frank, and James Lea Cate, eds. *The Army Air Forces in World War II*. Vol. 4: *The Pacific: Guadalcanal to Saipan, August 1942 to July 1944*. Washington, D.C.: Office of Air Force History, 1950.
Drea, Edward J. *MacArthur's ULTRA: Codebreaking and the War against Japan, 1942–1945*. Lawrence: University Press of Kansas, 1992.
Edoin, Hoito. *The Night Tokyo Burned*. New York: St. Martin's Press, 1987.
Eichelberger, Robert L. *Dear Miss Em: General Eichelberger's War in the Pacific, 1942–1945*. Edited by Jay Luvaas. Westport: Greenwood Press, 1972.
Eichelberger, Robert L., and Milton MacKaye. *Our Jungle Road to Tokyo*. New York: Viking Press, 1950.
Ellis, John. *The Sharp End: The Fighting Man in World War II*. New York: Charles Scribner's Sons, 1980.
Harper, Stephen. *Miracle of Deliverance: The Case for the Bombing of Hiroshima and Nagasaki*. New York: Stein and Day Publishers, 1986.
James, D. Clayton. *The Years of MacArthur*. Vol. 2: *1941–1945*. Boston: Houghton Mifflin Company, 1975.
Kahn, Sy M. *Between Tedium and Terror: A Soldier's World War II Diary, 1943–1945*. Urbana and Chicago: University of Illinois Press, 1993.
Kennett, Lee B. *G.I.: The American Soldier in World War II*. New York: Charles Scribner's Sons, 1987.
McCartney, William F. *The Jungleers: A History of the 41st Infantry Division*. Washington: Infantry Journal Press, 1948.
McManus, John C. *The Deadly Brotherhood: The American Combat Soldier in World War II*. Novato, Calif.: Presidio Press, 1998.
Morison, Samuel Eliot. *New Guinea and the Marianas*. Vol. 8 of *History of United States Naval Operations in World War II*. Boston: Little, Brown and Company, 1953.
———. *The Liberation of the Philippines: Luzon, Mindanao, the Visayas, 1944–1945*. Vol. 13 of *History of United States Naval Operations in World War II*. Boston: Little, Brown and Company, 1959.
Sherrod, Robert. *History of Marine Corps Aviation in World War II*. Baltimore, Md.: Nautical and Aviation Publishing Company of America, 1987.
Shortal, John F. *Forged by Fire: General Robert L. Eichelberger and the Pacific War*. Columbia: University of South Carolina Press, 1987.

Smith, Robert Ross. *The Approach to the Philippines.* United States Army in World War
   II. The War in the Pacific. Washington, D.C.: Office of the Chief of Military His-
   tory, Department of the Army, 1953.
————. *Triumph in the Philippines.* United States Army in World War II. The War in
   the Pacific. Washington, D.C.: Center of Military History, U.S. Army, 1963.
Spector, Ronald H. *Eagle against the Sun: The American War with Japan.* New York:
   The Free Press, 1985.
Taaffe, Stephen R. *MacArthur's Jungle War.* Lawrence: University Press of Kansas,
   1998.
Westerfield, Hargis. *41st Infantry Division: Fighting Jungleers.* Paducah, Ky.: Turner
   Publishing Company, 1992.
Young, Peter, ed. *The World Almanac of World War II.* New York: Scripps-Howard
   Company, 1981.

INDEX

After receiving his discharge from the U.S. Army, **Francis B. Catanzaro** attended St. Louis University, where he earned a B.S. in Chemistry. He then married the girl across the street. They have three children and seven grandchildren. He spent most of his business career with Boise Cascade, where he was employed as Quality Assurance Manager and Laboratory Manager of the Packaging Division.